Private Pain

Rich Wilkerson

with Helen Hosier

HARVEST HOUSE PUBLISHERS
Eugene, Oregon 97402

PRIVATE PAIN

Copyright © 1987 by Harvest House Publishers
Eugene, Oregon 97402

Library of Congress Catalog Card Number 87-081047
ISBN 0-89081-620-4

To my mother, Bonnie Wilkerson,
and my mother-in-law, Lorraine Buntain.
These two people have known private pain
and have demonstrated the character
of Christ through it all.

Acknowledgments

First of all I praise the Lord for allowing me to be in His service.

Special thanks to Helen Hosier for her editorial assistance. Also special thanks to Rose Haney for her manuscript preparation. Finally, special thanks to the Hawkins family and all of my friends at Harvest House.

Preface

It is my privilege to travel North America as an evangelist for Jesus Christ. During one of my crusades, a middle-aged gentleman approached me and asked if we could get together the next day. He wanted me to pray with him concerning a personal problem.

The next afternoon when I met with him, he related the following story. Years before, he had been a member of a gospel singing team from Europe. As he continued to recount his story, I remembered who he was.

He told me how God had blessed the team here in America, and how after the group had disbanded he had married a beautiful pastor's daughter from his country. Shortly after the birth of their only child, they moved to Canada.

At this point he began to cry and said, "Rich, I've always loved the Lord, but what has happened to me has stretched my faith to the very limits."

After their only child entered elementary school, his wife decided she wanted a job. She did very well in her work and was promoted to a better position within the company.

It was in the fifth year of her employment that he noticed a change in his wife's behavior. He said her affection toward him left their relationship. She began phoning home at dinner time to say she had to work overtime. But when he tried to reach her later in the evening, she was never there.

He suspected another man. When he finally had the evidence to confront her, she confessed to the affair. But because of their strict upbringing, neither one of them could file for divorce. They continued to share the same house, but his wife's lover took an apartment across the street.

His wife is at home in the morning to make breakfast for their 12-year-old daughter and is there in the afternoon when the daughter arrives home. His wife makes dinner and stays with their daughter until he arrives home in the evening.

"The moment I walk in the door I watch my wife leave the house and walk across the street into the arms of her boyfriend. I know she won't be home until 6 A.M.

"I wish I could just walk away, Rich, but I love her and so does my daughter. It's a tough way to try and keep a family together," he said.

"Not possible," you say? I tell you that I am learning every day that truth is truly stranger than fiction. This is just another word picture of a family living with private pain.

I have endeavored through this book to help those who are facing problems in their lives—personal, unspoken kinds of problems. The painful, embarrassing kind.

What is your private pain? For two thousand years Jesus has been in the business of healing private pain. I'm happy to report that He is still in business. His words still ring true today: "Come unto me, all ye that labour and are heavy laden, and I will give you rest" (Matthew 11:28 KJV).

I trust that you will find rest for your weary soul through the reading of this book.

—Rich Wilkerson
Tacoma, Washington

Contents

Private Pain

Section I

PORTRAITS OF PRIVATE PAIN
WE DO NOT UNVEIL

"AM I A GOD NEAR AT HAND,"
SAYS THE LORD,
"AND NOT A GOD AFAR OFF?
CAN ANYONE HIDE HIMSELF IN SECRET PLACES,
SO I SHALL NOT SEE HIM?"
SAYS THE LORD;
"DO I NOT FILL HEAVEN AND EARTH?"

JEREMIAH 23:23,24

Chapter 1

THE PAIN WE DON'T TALK ABOUT

> Down through the ages, the prophets and the
> saints have given witness to the fact that God
> helps those who trust Him. . . .
> —Warren W. Wiersbe[1]

Private pain. You identified with the title, that's why you
are reading this book. You don't need anyone to define what
private pain is. You know. Oh, how you know! You know
only too well. And now someone has written a book about
those things you have found too painful to discuss. You have
discovered that it is far easier to carry the burden without
the advice of others, however well-intentioned such advice
might be. For the most part, the ache in your heart is yours
alone.

Private pain suggests embarrassment, inner anguish, rup-
tured relationships, emotional isolation, rejection, disappointment, aloneness, suppressed anger, and depression. It
may mean child or wife abuse, incest, cruelty, verbal abuse,
a poor self-image, fear, discouragement, criticism, disillusionment with friends or a family member, some personal
vendetta with you as the target, overwhelming financial
difficulties, loss of job, career dissatisfaction, or bondage to
an enslaving addiction, and guilt.

Private pain summons unanswered questions. Many of
you live with uncomfortable "If onlys" and "What ifs" that

test your faith. You don't like the feelings your painful wonderings produce.

Private pain can be physical, psychological, material, emotional, intellectual, or cultural. There are no cultural or geographical barriers. It's a universal problem with no age limits. Even little children experience private pain. I know something about the private pain that young people experience.

When I spoke to one high school assembly, two thousand kids jammed into the gymnasium. Halfway through, I lightly touched on the subject of abortion. I just mentioned the word—just a brief reference to this painful subject—and a girl began screaming. A shocked audience watched as she staggered out of the bleachers, weeping uncontrollably. I finished speaking, but afterwards, when I went to the principal's office, she was there, still crying.

"I'm sorry I created such a disturbance," she apologized between her sobs. "Two years ago when I was 14 I had an abortion. No one ever told me about the kind of hell I'd live with the rest of my life. Every morning I wake up thinking about it. Every night before I go to bed, it's on my mind. I live with such terrible pain and guilt. When you mentioned that word this morning, I couldn't handle it."

That teenage girl was suffering with a lot of private pain.

Since 1971 there have been over 20 million abortions performed in our country. That means there are literally millions of women suffering from guilt and depression.

Since that day, I have encountered many of these young girls, as well as young, middle-aged, and older women who have related the guilt and private pain they live with as a result of an abortion. Post-abortion trauma is a soul-searing experience.

Private pain is usually more emotional than physical. However, private pain can be physical, too. I first stumbled onto the reality of private pain as I dealt with individuals across the country. In my own mind I identified it as "private pain." After such encounters, I'd hear myself saying,

"Private pain . . . more private pain . . . private pain."

Rarely did these individuals reveal the reason for their inner anguish to those around them. But I was an evangelist. I wouldn't be around to remind them that someone else knew! They'd wait on the fringes while I talked to others and then timidly say, "Mr. Wilkerson, may I have a word with you?"

But how much can you reveal in a few moments with a crowd milling around you?

Jesus could tell you. In one brief moment of time, a woman in a crowd managed to inch her way through to Him. Did she crawl on her hands and knees? We can't be certain. The biblical record provides some evidence that she might have. But could she crawl through a throng and not be crushed? She came close enough to stretch out her hand to touch Him. He was almost within reach.

She must have thought, *I'm so close . . . I can't let Him get away without at least touching Him.* She tried a little harder . . . *yes, oh yes, ohhh,* she was inwardly groaning. "Yes! Thank God! Yes! I touched Him . . . I touched Him! I touched the hem of His garment!"

The Touch That Heals

The woman's story is a magnificent account—but first, a little background. Jesus was on His way to heal someone else. A father's impassioned cry for his dying daughter had moved the heart of Jesus. Jairus had fallen at Jesus' feet, crying, "Come to my house. My daughter is dying." The man was a ruler of the synagogue, which made his request all the more unusual. Synagogue leaders rarely had anything to do with this man Jesus.

And so as Jesus walked along with Jairus, the man's little daughter was dying. The crowds that always followed Jesus were no different that day, except that perhaps Jesus was trying to move a little faster to comply with Jairus' urgent request.

Although the need was great, the procession was slow because "the people thronged him" (Luke 8:42 KJV). Then, He felt the touch. Incredible! Multitudes pressing against Him, yet He felt a special tug on the hem of His garment. "Who touched me?" Denials all around. No one admitted he'd touched Him.

"Master, the multitudes throng You and press You, and You say, 'Who touched Me?' " Peter said.

And Jesus answered, "Somebody touched Me, for I perceived power going out from Me" (Luke 8:45,46).

The woman knew at once that what she'd done couldn't be hidden from Jesus. She came trembling, falling down before Him, and "she declared to Him in the presence of all the people the reason she had touched Him and how she was healed immediately" (v. 47).

No longer was her embarrassment and pain private. Women can easily understand this woman's reluctance to talk about her problem. It was a woman's kind of problem. A physical problem, but also an emotional problem. She'd lived with it 12 years (see also Matthew 9:20 and Mark 5:25). Modesty prevented her from coming right out with her request for healing. Moreover, she'd already made the rounds of all the physicians and no one had been able to help her (see Luke 8:43). It was imperative that her private pain remain a secret for she was considered ceremonially unclean. This kind of problem excommunicated her from the services of the synagogue, and thus shut her out from the women's courts in the temple. But it didn't cut her off from approaching Christ the Healer. Hers was indeed a pathetic figure!

The Impulse of the Spirit of Faith

By a wonderful impulse of the Spirit of faith, this woman believed that Jesus had an overflowing healing virtue. To herself she declared: "If only I may touch His garment, I shall be made well" (Matthew 9:21).

We need to learn what this woman accepted by faith—there is such virtue, such fullness of grace in Christ, such favor that no one need fear reaching out to Him. She stole a cure, thinking it would go unnoticed. She was ready to be gone and on her way, but Christ wasn't willing to let her go. And there's something in that unwillingness on His part that we must notice. "Daughter," Jesus said, "Be of good cheer; your faith has made you well. Go in peace" (Luke 8:48).

Has Jesus comforted you in your moments of private pain? Even though the pain may still be there—or your particular problem hasn't changed—has He made it more bearable for you?

A lot of private pain in Christian circles is caused by the fiery tongue—sometimes by false accusations. The tongue is a fire, as the apostle James wrote; out of control it can do a lot of damage (see James 3). It can sever friendships, destroy families, split churches, leave gaping wounds in the hearts of the victims. How do you handle that kind of private pain? How does Jesus comfort you when you're falsely accused?

We can be crushed by false accusations or we can rise above them. One friend who experienced the private pain of a false accusation refused to be destroyed by it. The accusation was absolutely untrue so she went back, confronted her accuser, and told him, "You owe me an apology. You need to set the record straight. What you have done is very painful to me."

There was no apology. Rather, her accuser stuck by his story. Even though he persisted in malicious gossip, my friend had a clear conscience. She was innocent—wounded, but innocent. Like the woman who touched the hem of Christ's garment, my friend reached out to Jesus. God comforted her and poured the comfort of His love into her wounded heart. She was able to stand up and walk away from that encounter, comforted by God, guiltless, and set free from the private pain that had shattered her at first.

What happened to her accuser, the man who had misjudged her? Nothing. He did not apologize but eventually he discontinued his slander. He knew that he was in the wrong and was silenced by his own guilt.

And what did my friend do? She could have made it embarrassing for him. She chose not to do so. God had vindicated her; she did not retaliate. She chose not to subject her accuser to that kind of pain.

Have you come to terms with your private pain? Have your long years of praying about a certain situation been answered? But have you gone on your way without acknowledging God's help to others? It's an encouragement to others when we share what Jesus has done for us.

God gives peace as He did for the woman who touched the hem of His garment. He told her to be of good cheer. *He never lets us just go.* He gave her an encouraging word so that she could go on her way cheered and peaceful, and others would see her and recognize the change. When we know that things are right between God and us, we radiate the peace He gives.

I've known people whose circumstances are very difficult and painful. But pain isn't what you see on their faces. It's peace. Christians should communicate their experiences to one another as a means of encouraging others to trust Him. We are to comfort others with the comfort wherewith we have been comforted.

When He honors our faith, we honor Him by giving a good report of it, even if it means swallowing our pride. Christ will be pleased if we are willing to do that for Him. The woman who touched the hem of Christ's garment received a physical, as well as a spiritual healing. Her faith brought it about. Now she was really whole.

Imagine how she must have felt, as she went her way, reflecting, "He called me 'Daughter,' He healed me! He honored my faith!"

There is nothing hidden from the all-seeing eye of the Father. Your pain may be so grievous that you don't want to expose it to all the world, but you can't keep it from God. We need to learn what God said to the prophet Jeremiah. He is not a God who is afar off; He is always near at hand. He can remove the cause of your private pain or He can give you the grace to live with it. Regardless of the means, the method, or the result of your coming to Him, your faith need not be diminished. God has His reasons. To be chosen to bear private pain for Him is to be counted worthy and special to the Father. Pour out your heart before Him; your fear and trembling present no barriers to Him. This woman's story—the woman who touched Christ's garment—is the story of private pain. Her condition is mirrored in the private pain that stalks this world like an invasive cancer. It invades our neighborhoods, churches, schools, businesses, and homes. It attacks the wealthy as well as the poor. Few are exempt from some degree of private pain.

As I read this woman's story, I wondered what caused her to lead a life of private pain, a life characterized by loneliness and shame. These factors plague countless people in our society today. We will examine these factors in the succeeding chapters.

This woman could not know that her story would witness to generations to come of God's faithfulness to those who trust in Him. I'm glad she dared to approach Him, furtive as that approach may have been. It says much to me about Jesus' understanding of the private pain you and I harbor, and of His willingness to heal whether the pain be physical, emotional, or spiritual.

Ponder this truth: God will give you the faith you need to be patient while He works out His perfect plan for your life. "So if you are suffering according to God's will, keep on doing what is right and trust yourself to the God who made you, for he will never fail you" (1 Peter 4:19 TLB).

> We touch Him in life's throng and press
> And we are whole again.
> —G. Campbell Morgan

CHAPTER 2

THE INSIGNIFICANT FACTOR:

One Is Such a Lonely Number

> He who consciously or unconsciously has cho-
> sen to ignore God is an orphan in the uni-
> verse. . . .
>
> —Emile Cailliet[1]

Loneliness is the price we mortals pay for noninvolve-
ment. Whatever our reasons for seclusion or failure to become a part of the mainstream of our particular world, we
will suffer the consequences of aloneness. Not all "aloneness" is bad—some people value their solitude as a creative
force for good in their lives. But lonely aloneness stabs at the
heart.

It was the poet Milton who said, "Loneliness is the first
thing which God's eye named as not good." A worldwide
hunger for love and acceptance is behind many bizarre
activities: experimenting with drugs, sex, the occult, weird-
looking dress. These actually produce more agony and
heartache, more loneliness in the long run.

We were not created to function alone. We long for com-
munication—someone in whom we can confide, someone
who understands and accepts us, someone we can trust,
someone with whom we can let the barriers down and relax.
Psychological studies and testing prove that loneliness is
one of mankind's greatest fears. Meaningful relationships
with other people are a fundamental need.

Our supreme need is for the fellowship we can have with

the Liberator. Billy Graham says: "Man was made for God and without God he is going to be lonely. . . . His sins, the Bible says, have separated him from God. Man thinks if he indulges in acts of pleasure he can drown his feeling of loneliness; but nothing works apart from God. The thing we are longing for is the thing we were made for."

The loneliness of being without a home or being friendless, the loneliness of success or failure, the loneliness of being misunderstood or not even understanding one's self, the loneliness of old age, the loneliness of wives, husbands, children, and youth all spell private pain. It also describes the loneliness of the woman with the issue of blood—the one who touched the hem of Jesus' garment.

She was poor. Weak. Friendless. Unknown. Lonely. Her life was darkened by continual suffering and disease—a disease that made her ceremonially unclean in the culture of her day, an outcast from society. A piteous case.

In today's culture we do not fully appreciate this woman's weakness and sorrow, nor the extent of her plight. Not only did the Hebrew economy prevent this woman from taking any part or place in the worship of God if she was married, but she was divorced from her husband by the same law. She was literally ostracized from society.

We don't deal with that kind of law today; thank God it's passed away forever. For the most part, in today's culture we are more compassionate. Society (at least this society) seeks ways to take care of the helpless and those who are suffering and there are families who do not turn their backs on their own.

Portraits of Pain We Do Not Unveil

Even so, this kind of woman is plentiful. They roam the streets of our cities. Forlorn. Rejected. Penniless. Quite often they sit hunched in rest homes, retirement centers, hospices—abandoned, to all intents and purposes, by their families.

They occupy the pews in churches across the land, many of them well-dressed, intelligent, but oh, so lonely.

They sit on boards of great corporations; they occupy positions of influence.

They go home at night to mansions, condominiums, apartments, and houses. Lonely. They share their private lives with few, if any others. They know the meaning of private pain.

Some have no home. They sleep over grates in city streets, or they find a haven in some downtown shelter. Others eke out a bare living and exist in squalor.

They have one thing in common with the woman who made her way through the throngs to Jesus. They are one in a crowd, their private inner pain unnoticed by others.

For generations the miraculous healing of this woman has been preached all over the world by ministers of the gospel. Doubtless her story has inspired thousands of miracles as Christ has responded to the demonstration of faith. But in the context of Scripture, it almost appears as a "secondary miracle." The woman's healing happened on the way to another miracle—the raising of the dead daughter of Jairus. Ask a group of people which was the more miraculous of the two and you might get some surprising answers. But a miracle is a miracle. Can one surpass the other?

Our Sense of Desperate Need

Here was a woman so ashamed of her private pain that she secretly hoped to steal a mmiracle cure without anyone finding out. Both Jairus and this woman shared the consciousness of desperate need. No human help had been of any value.

Even today we seek every possible means to effect a cure for our problems, whatever they may be. Like the woman and Jairus, we come to Christ as our last resort. Think about it. How sad! But even though we come to Him as our last refuge, of this we can be sure: Christ is always a safe refuge.

Harry Blamires calls our attention to this with his insightful statement: "How desperate, how tragic, is a man's situation when, all other resources exhausted, he is thrown back upon eternal God! That is the attitude that confronts us today," Blamires says. "The acts of God are known—but on the very fringe of things knowable. The knowledge of God's power is stored in the memory along with other data accumulated against a possible rainy day. . . . But immediately applicable? Relevant to me, here, now. . . . Thank God . . . no."[2]

Sound familiar? Why do individuals resist coming to God for the help they need when He is so available? There isn't an act of our lives that we commit, simple or profound, whereby we aren't actively fulfilling God's will or opposing God's will. "You are God's child, obedient or disobedient. In your every thought, every plan, every uttered word, God is active or God is resisted. . . . God is not on the fringe of life: He is in the dead center, at every moment resisted or obeyed."[3]

There are excuses and there are reasons why people ignore the help of the Father. The reasons may be, to some extent, legitimate when there is ignorance of the Father's resources. It is difficult to comprehend that, with churches on street corners throughout the land and mass media being used by pastors and evangelists, individuals exist who know little or nothing of t1he miracle-working power of God. There are still those who have never had a personal encounter with the reality of Jesus Christ.

What about the private pain of the unredeemed—the God-rejecting, God-ignorant man or woman, boy or girl who has never settled the eternal question of sin and separation from God? What of the man who, knowing the claims of Christ, nevertheless builds his stock receipts and rises to the top of the corporation at the cost of eternity? Or consider the woman who, knowing the story of Jesus, chooses to harden her heart for more appealing secular causes or world acclaim. Think of the person who, though shuffling past the other side of 80, has never heard about the simple act of the woman who touched the hem of Christ's garment—the elderly one who has never pressed the throng to reach the Savior. And what of the child who has never heard the name of Jesus apart from a curse word or an expletive? What about the business man or woman numbed by cocaine or other drugs and the alcoholic teenager bound by the rules of his peers? And consider those around the world who do not have churches on every corner (and no street corners) or Bibles in every home; yet they have that private inner pain that tells them that something—SOMEONE—is missing in their lives. Or what of the unredeemed who amass silver and gold, wield power and authority, yet hide the private pain that is sending hay, wood, and stubble into eternity?

And if these—the unredeemed—cannot reach out (or will not reach out) to the Savior themselves, then we should reach out for them. Like Jairus, the synagogue ruler, who sought Jesus on behalf of his dying child. Like the father of the prodigal who surely kept watch for the homecoming of his wayward son. And like the lonely woman who allowed herself to be caught up with the throng that followed Jesus. In each case, surely Jesus stopped, saw the need, responded, and took eternal joy in having virtue go out of Him that someone else might be redeemed.

The private pain of the unredeemed is indescribable. Many of us have already walked that route with emotions as varying as the depths of the sea. Private pain, like living hell, sears our soul, deadens our conscience, mars our dreams, and leaves us empty, guilt-ridden, bound, purposeless, suicidal, and spiritually dead. The indifference or rejection or outward appearance of the unredeemed should not block our efforts to reach out to them. Then they, in turn, may reach out to the redemptive love provided by God through a simple Galilean who walked dusty roads, proclaimed a life-giving message, wore a crown of thorns, hung on a painful, lonely cross, and left a stone-heewn tomb to return to glory.

A 15-year-old girl came to the altar one night in a crusade on the east coast. She was emaciated, disheveled, and looked at the point of death. She had lived on the streets for three months. We talked after she came to faith in Christ that night.

Kelly had never heard of a God who loved her. She told me that she came to the altar because I had said that God will forgive people for any and everything. Furthermore, once forgiven, God will no longer hold the sin against a person's record again. It's forgiven and forgotten.

During her time on the streets she had committed all kinds of terrible sins. She was ashamed of what she had done. She couldn't bear to face her family and least of all darken the door of a church.

"But tonight my embarrassment was no longer holding me back," she said. "God really does love me. He really has forgiven me. He is no longer holding my past against me!"

The story doesn't end there. Three years later, I was speaking at an evening convention in the same area. Before I spoke, a group of eight singers from a nearby Christian college sang. While they were singing, I noticed the girl at the end of the ensemble. Her countenance radiated through the entire performance. I could see that she truly loved the God of whom she was singing. At the end of the conference she and her friends walked up to me. "My name is Kelly," she told me. "Three years ago I was living on the streets, then I went to your crusade. I found peace with God that night, Mr. Wilkerson, and I was forever changed by His grace."

I was thrilled to see the love of God so marvelously displayed in her life. Now she was in her second year of college, preparing to be a missionary. If God can take the embarrassment, sin, and shame away from someone like Kelly, He can do it for anybody.

But the excuses are something else! We are so excuse-prone. The apostle Paul reminds us that since the creation of the world, God's invisible attributes are clearly seen in the earth, the sky, and all that He has made. Instinctively we know that there is great eternal power behind creation alone. Paul says those who push the truth away from them, who ignore these evidences of His power, "they are without excuse" (Romans 1:20).

Even the uninformed are treading in dangerous water by their failure to acknowledge truths that can be readily discernible. Theologian Emile Cailliet points out that what God has initiated and given cannot be ignored; such self-centered denial of God's distinctive endowment characterizes sin, and he who consciously or unconsciously chooses to ignore God is an orphan in the universe. Paul says "their senseless minds are darkened."

Satan's Lie Believed

Believing Satan's lie is the great tragedy for those who live with the burden of private pain.

Satan, that devious adversary, caused the woman with an issue of blood to believe that the help of God was unavailable to her. Excluded from church participation because of her uncleanness, she was ignorant of Old Testament truth relating to God's mercy.

She must have been watching from the fringes as Jesus went about doing good, healing people—performing miracle after miracle—and showing kindness and tender mercy to those the religious leaders scorned. Yes, she must have been watching Him.

Can you imagine her sneaking along, afraid to mingle with the crowds, pulling her clothes around her, attempting to withdraw into herself? Can you picture her hiding behind trees or between buildings, just to get a glimpse of this man? Inside she responded to what she was seeing. Hope rose within her. And faith.

The woman saw Jesus to be the Son of God. Her faith was beautifully suited to her particular circumstances. Such is the nature of the Father-heart of God. That spark of belief, hope, and faith produced a wonderful effect because God honors faith. Remember what Jesus said: If we had faith even as a grain of mustard seed we could remove mountains (see Matthew 17:20).

A mustard seed is the tiniest of seeds. It wasn't the quantity of her faith, or your faith or mine that counts; it was and is the quality. But Satan would keep you bound in the stranglehold of disbelief, shackled by private pain.

And so the woman came. Hope would have its way. Faith would have its reward.

One Is Such a Lonely Number

No longer would she suffer the pangs of loneliness that were all too familiar to her during those long, lonely years. After her miraculous healing she could venture forth as one saved, radiant in the discoveries of God's grace and mercy, eager to share her newfound joy. Jesus had told her to be of good cheer. To go out in peace. She was a blessed woman. Did she know the Old Testament proverb that said, "The blessing of the Lord makes one rich" (Proverbs 10:22)? How richly blessed she was!

I like to think she knew it. She recognized it. I look forward to meeting that blessed woman in heaven someday. I want to know more—how did her life change from that moment on? Did she go about sharing her miracle of healing and the joy of the Lord? How did this joy dispel the darkness in heer soul and the sadness in her previously lonely hours?

Perhaps she became one of Jesus' closest followers. Maybe she was one of the women at the foot of the cross or one of the women who came to the tomb early on the morning following Jesus' crucifixion. Was she an active part of the early church? Surely her life became vastly different. She would no longer suffer the private pain of unutterable loneliness and despair.

I was sitting on the stage of a large church one Sunday morning. As we sang a hymn, I looked down to the people on the front row. My gaze settled on a beautiful family—a mother and six children.

The oldest son, a 14-year-old, sat next to his mother. The youngest—a two-year-old—sat at the far end away from his mother. Those six children sat absolutely still for the entire service. I was amazed! I said to the pastor, "What a family that is, sitting on the front row."

The pastor answered back, "What a story!"

Later, in his office, the pastor told me, "Two years ago while the mother was pregnant with the two-year-old, her husband—the father of the six children—was imprisoned for 25 years for repeatedly raping the five older children.

"Each morning that woman arises at 4:30 A.M., makes the breakfast, and gets the kids ready for school. Then she drops two of them at the daycare center, two at the elementary school, and two at the junior high school. She gets to work by 8:00 A.M. She picks them up after work and goes to her lonely home for dinner. She's living on a shoestring, but they're making it. Recently she told me that Sunday is the only day she has free. But she still gets up at 4:30 A.M. to get the family ready for Sunday school.

"She says this church, by its love for Jesus, has provided the only real companionship she has. Her boys have met godly men who treat them like their own sons. Her daughter, too, has found love.

"But, Rich, if you were here tonight and this coming Wednesday night, you would see that family sitting in the same row. This is their second home."

When I got back to my hotel room that afternoon, I knelt by my bed and thought of this woman's private pain. But I also thanked God for giving her hope in place of despair.

And that's what friendship with Jesus does for those who touch Him. The loneliness and despair that may be your constant companion are known to Him. He can fill up the lonely gaps in your life.

Perhaps you are still mourning the recent loss of a loved one, or you may have lost your life's partner years ago yet still feel his or her absence. According to Edith Schaeffer, death is an ugly ripping apart of what is meant to be together. It's not what God intended for His creation, but Lucifer triumphed in the Garden with our first parents. Mankind has lived with the effects of that first sin ever since. Death is part of the ongoing battle between Satan and God. But be assured, the final victory is God's.

Meanwhile, those who loved much suffer the loss and that's deep private pain.

Sometime back, my wife and I received a phone call from a church member where we had previously served. She was calling to tell us about a young man we knew who really loved the Lord. He came from a fine Christian family. This young man was a tremendous witness for the Lord and led many of his friends to Christ. He was a leader of the street-witnessing teams, had a fabulous singing voice, and was loved by all.

About a year after my wife and I accepted the call to another church, this young man moved away to attend college. While there, he became entangled in the gay community.

The woman who called us said, "Rich, several months ago he came home looking very ill. His parents put him in the hospital only to discover their son had AIDS. They were so emotionally disturbed by this that they put a strict quarantine on all visitors wanting to see their son.

"I don't really know if they'll ever recover, Rich. They are so brokenhearted that they themselves are looking ill. I did hear that their boy repented of his sin. But, Rich, he passed away two days ago."

My heart ached as I thought back to what a wonderful young man he had been. I grieved for the parents and the shame and private pain they were experiencing. But then the Lord spoke to my heart and said, "I can forgive anyone, Rich. His parents will see him again if they trust Me." God can even forgive an AIDS patient and take him to heaven.

I cannot move on without reminding you who bear the private pain of losing a loved one, that your loss is heaven's gain when that loved one is a child of God (see 2 Corinthians 5:8). Let that be your comfort for now and share it with others. This in itself will work a miracle of healing for you as you demonstrate your faith.

You may be someone who comes home from work at night to your lonely apartment or house. Or you may be retired, your days one long succession of lonely hours broken only now and then with outside involvement. You long to share life with someone. One is such a lonely number.

Jesus doesn't want you to go through life alone and friendless. The Bible says there is a friend that sticketh closer than a brother, and that friend is Jesus. Marriage may not necessarily be the answer, for not everyone chooses to marry, but the companionship and friendship of others is desirable. It's doubtful that the woman who touched the hem of Jesus' garment and experienced healing had a husband or friends.

We don't know if this woman was married or not, or even how old she was. For just a moment let's assume that she was unmarried and that she longed for a marriage partner with whom she could share life at its most intimate level. The aloneness she felt would have been compounded by her desire to bear children—all the instincts common to a woman.

I believe there was something of compelling desire as she reached out to touch the hem of Jesus' garment. For 12 long years she'd watched former friends marry, bear and rear their children. She'd been deprived of those joys. The depth of her sorrow we can scarcely comprehend. But it was so pathetically real.

I do not think like a woman, but I have a wife, a mother, and sisters. Together my wife and I have counseled troubled women through the years—women bearing crushing loads of private pain. I know enough about the emotions of women to realize that the hemorrhaging woman was absolutely desolate. During 12 years of physical, mental, and spiritual agony, she poured out her all in an attempt to regain her health, with no success.

In the case of Jairus, he and his wife had enjoyed 12 years of sunshine with their precious daughter. Now it appeared that their joy was to be snatched away by that cruelest of all enemies, death. But with the woman, it had been 12 years of suffering that had weakened her to the point of utter desolation.

Let's suppose that at one time she had been married. He'd divorced her. And he was justified in his actions by the law of the land. Compounded tragedy! In her culture she could not even live in her own home. She couldn't even mother their children if, indeed, she'd borne children before she was afflicted. She couldn't even touch them. Furthermore, no human being was allowed to touch her. Imagine going without the touch of someone you love! Her tears were the only thing that ever touched her face. Tradition had added to the hygiene of the law; it was a positive brutality.

Why the rigid law? It was believed that a woman suffering from hemorrhage (and that is the meaning of the Greek word used in these gospel passages) suffered as the result of personal immorality. Of course, it was an absolutely false conception and the Levitical code did not teach that; but it was the entrenched view of that time. The code did say that such a woman was to be segregated and that was in harmony with their beliefs.

It appears, however, that because of the length of her malady they believed her disease proved her immorality.

Supposition. And so she was treated as a pariah, a scarlet woman. Certainly all this played havoc with her emotions.

One woman conveyed to me the desolation she felt as a result of her divorce—a divorce that took place many years ago. The Christian community who knew her well, by virtue of her accomplishments, still falsely misjudged her. Supposition. Today's scarlet woman. There are many victims of vicious tongues falsely condemned by the unknowing judgmental public. Their pain is private and real.

And oh, the private pain of men and women whose marriages are sub-ideal! Marriages in name only. Husbands and wives staying together for the sake of their children or because they do not believe in divorce, yet seeking no way to reconcile their differences. A private war goes on constantly between them while they put on a good front in the presence of friends and the church. Pretense. What loneliness they endure! Such portraits of private pain are all too common in today's culture. They are all around us. Perhaps this describes you.

Some of the most lonely people in the world are the victims of divorce. Men whose wives have left them in pursuit of a career or another man; women whose husbands have abandoned them for another woman. Individuals who have opted for divorce rather than to continue living a lie. With one out of every two marriages ending in divorce, the pain being experienced at all levels of society and among every age group is staggering.

In the summer of 1986 I was holding evangelistic crusades in Mexico City. Nearly 50 people from nine different states went with us to plant a new church for the glory of God.

Several Christian colleges sent students to do pre-crusade preparation. We gathered the first night in a hotel for prayer. As I spoke to the workers, I spotted a man in his early fifties whom I recognized. I had no idea he would be joining us for the crusade. After my message and a great time of prayer, the workers headed back to their rooms. I made my way through the group to my friend. We exchanged greetings and embraced.

I had not seen him for nearly three years so I asked how his wife and family were doing. His shoulders sagged. "Didn't you hear, Rich? My wife walked out on me two years ago."

I was shocked! His wife was a model Christian—a compassionate lover of little children. She would gather them around her and teach them about Jesus.

He went on to say that she had left him for another man and had taken their children. "For six months I just sat in my living room every day after work crying until late at night.

"One day someone invited me to go on a missionary outreach to Mexico. I had lots of vacation time and so I went. Rich, it was the only thing that could get my mind off of my desperate situation.

"You just can't know how lonely I've been and how I've wept. But sharing Christ with those who have never heard has begun the healing process. Now I come down every six months for two weeks to witness to the saving grace of Jesus. When I heard you were starting a church, I wanted to help."

You Are Not Insignificant to the Father

What is the answer? It is to see ourselves as persons of worth. We are not insignificant zeros to the Father. We are not faceless nothings. We are of value. If you doubt that, try counting the hairs in your comb or brush the next time you do your hair. Yet, difficult as it is for you to count them, the Bible assures you that the very hairs of your head are numbered (see Luke 12:7).

That verse speaks to me of God's love and care. And because He cares, He is approachable. Jesus knew that the woman had deliberately touched Him even when He was being pressured and touched by the throng shoving against

Him as He walked along the road. That speaks convincingly of His awareness of you and me today.

In your private pain, let the consolation of His care sweep over you. You matter to Him. He longs to comfort you, to walk alongside you. Self-imposed isolation is not needful nor is it emotionally healthy. God wants to move in from the outskirts of the daily-ness of your living, to the center of your being where He can infuse you with life and hope and a reason for living. From the silence of your shame or the bitterness of your battle, remove the barriers and, like the anguished woman, reach out and touch Him. Invisible though He is to your seeing, let the eye of faith, small as it may be, move in His direction. He *will* respond. God longs to free you from the prison of your private pain.

Ponder this truth: Three times in the Old Testament, we hear this expression, "the apple of [my] eye." It is convincing evidence that God is involved in the lives of His children (see Deuteronomy 32:10, Psalm 17:8, and Zechariah 2:8). Moses, David, and Zechariah speak of this. Does that sound insignificant to you? That is an old expression that indicates favor and the deep caring of someone. In these instances, God was saying His children are "the apple of [my] eye."

Satan would like to undermine and destroy you just as he attempted to do with Moses, Elijah, Jonah, and David. The Bible is very contemporary and these accounts were written for our benefit. Look into the psalms. In particular, hear David's cries out of the agony of his private pain in Psalm 25:18,20-22. Read Numbers 11:14,15 and hear Moses' lament. Study the book of Jonah and learn about the prophet who tried running away from God. Recognize that these men, like you, were very human and God understands all about our humanness. Remember, He became one of us so that He could identify with us.

The Bible says "Let us draw near [to Him] with a true heart in full assurance of faith. . . . Let us hold fast the confession of our hope without wavering, for He who promised is faithful" (Hebrews 10:22,23).

God sometimes shuts the door and shuts us in,
That He may speak, perchance through grief or
    pain,
And softly, heart to heart, above the din,
May tell some precious thought to us again.
                                    —Author Unknown

Chapter 3

THE RISK FACTOR:

*Rejection, a Psychological
Disturbance of Epidemic
Proportions*

> You have private silences of heart you cannot afford to ignore.
>
> —Wayne E. Oates[1]

As I travel this nation, I find men, women, young people, and children, who are silencing their ideals and compromising their convictions. Adults know they can't "eat" ideals, so they stop pursuing their dreams. They cave in to the societal demands and muffle their inner protest. They've risked before and where has it gotten them? Rejection.

Does any of this sound familiar? You may have experienced a job loss, or a demotion, or been bypassed for that promotion that was long overdue because you expressed your convictions. We fear going out on a limb. Memories of painful past experiences haunt us.

It happens in churches and organizations too. People stop expressing their views (convictions) because they've been hurt once too often. Embarrassing rejection.

Many people bear private pain as a result of maintaining their integrity, refusing to compromise. One person, who couldn't live a lie, made a decision that ostracized him from his church and most of his friends. He paid a heavy price, including the loss of his own 12-year-old business.

He risked and encountered rejection. However, in time he was able to make new friends, get back into the work he knew so well, and reconstruct his life. "I held before myself the example of Peter [in the Bible] who disappointed Jesus by his denial, but Jesus never gave up on Peter and I knew what I had done was acceptable with God. So while my friends and even my church didn't stand by me, God did. Being able to live with a clear conscience made their rejection more bearable. Disappointing, sure, but God gave me the strength and ability to handle it."

Listen to the heart cry in this letter that I received from a woman after our crusade in her city:

Dear Mr. Wilkerson,

When you were here, I attended five out of six of your meetings. The one that touched me the most was the one on private pain. I could not believe how it applied to me. I cried through your whole message and felt the final release of all my sins, guilt, and fear. I wanted to tell you my whole story after that message, but I had to leave. Now I must tell you my story. . . .

Between the ages of six and 19, I was 40-80 pounds over my normal weight. Finally, when I was 19, I went on the final diet of my life. I dropped 88 pounds in a little less than a year. It was all downhill from that point until now.

As I became more physically attractive, I began having dates. This was new to me. As I began dating, I began sleeping with all of the men of my life. I didn't understand what love meant. I felt that in order to be close to a man, I had to sleep with him. This ended a year ago. I've been engaged for nearly a year and am planning to get married in two months to a wonderful man I have known for about four years. We are saving intimacy for marriage. I know now what love really is. At 24 I know how to love and be loved.

Now here I was engaged to be married—something I had dreamed of since I was a little girl—and Satan was saying to me, "You are not going to make it to the wedding, you are not going to have a long life with your husband because of your past. *You have AIDS.*" This was not the case, but I was believing Satan's lie.

In October, 1986, four days before I took Jesus into my life, I was watching a morning news show that said heterosexuals can contract AIDS. Fear raced through me. All I could think about was having it. I was doomed I believed. In about ten minutes I was physically ill. I began vomiting and missed the next two days of work. The fear of having this dreaded disease consumed me.

The next day was my fiance's birthday. I could not even stand to be around people who loved me. That night, the AIDS fear was so heavy on my mind, I couldn't think of anything else. I couldn't sleep. Finally, I got up and called my in-laws-to-be.

My father-in-law-to-be answered the phone. I told him I couldn't sleep and had to talk to someone right away. He told me to come at once. When I got there, they were waiting at the door with the porch light on. I ran up to them and threw my arms around them and screamed, "Please help me!"

It was difficult to tell them about my past. Satan was telling me I was too insignificant, too bad to be forgiven. I made up my mind not to let Satan keep me from getting this private pain out in the open so it could be taken care of, no matter how embarrassing.

My story flowed out. I told them what I had done and how I feared AIDS. They didn't blink an eye but asked me if I was ready to accept Jesus Christ as my personal Savior. I said, "Oh yes! I know that is what I need." We prayed together until about 5:00 that morning. Tears kept coming.

I told them that Satan had put a picture in my mind: I was viewing my own funeral. My mother was there telling everyone what I had died of and that my husband (your son) was now infected. I knew in my heart Jesus was calling me to come to Him to get rid of the fear and guilt. Satan made me feel so dirty and used.

The next morning I went to church for the first time in years with my in-laws-to-be. When the pastor gave the altar call, I went forward. It was so wonderful; now I could live for Christ.

Since then, it has been an uphill climb. I must keep my focus on Jesus. At times though, Mr. Wilkerson, it has been hard. I am weak at times—especially when AIDS is in the news and flashed on TV all the time. It is like Satan taking his pitchfork and nudging me in the ribs and saying, "You are doomed." This only sends me through one more fear attack. It is during these times that I need the Lord the most. Sometimes I wish I was a little girl again, a virgin. I would change so many things. My father-in-law-to-be said I was a virgin again, because of 2 Corinthians 5:17. He says God has forgiven me and made me a brand-new person. My trouble is forgiving myself; I'm working on that now.

Your message on private pain hit home. I didn't think anyone could forgive me for what I had done. I have a new life now and will be married soon to someone who loves me more than life itself, and I love him. God bless you, Mr. Wilkerson. Please keep me in your prayers.

Your friend,
(name withheld)

The Tragedy of a Wasted Life

I think the woman who tried to remain incognito while grasping for the hem of Jesus' garment had experienced so much rejection in her lifetime that she feared another such encounter. Whether it was a journey to the marketplace or standing in the street in front of the synagogue, risk was always her companion.

The story of this forlorn woman is told in three of the gospel accounts. This indicates to me that there was something so memorable about this incident that each of the writers faithfully recorded it. There is more than meets the eye in this account. That is why I have chosen to examine her story in detail, for she, out of all the Bible stories, best exemplifies private pain.

With unflinching candor, each writer portrays certain aspects of her wasted life. But it is Mark who paints the episode with a touch of satire. The condition of the woman was hopeless, but Mark tells us she had "*suffered* many things from many physicians. She had spent all that she had and was no better, but rather grew worse" (Mark 5:26, emphasis mine). Small wonder that she despaired.

Do you feel the sting in Mark's descriptive words? This *abuse* at the hands of the doctors only added to her hopelessness and certainly fueled her mistrust of the human race in general. She had ended up a virtual pauper as her condition grew worse.

Have you endured much at the hands of someone who controls you? This is the idea behind Mark's graphic description. Perhaps it's at the hands of a repressive mate or ungrateful, manipulative children. Perhaps yours is or was a work-related situation.

I hear many discussions these days about the difficulties people encounter in their jobs. There is uncertainty and on-the-job stress with much backstabbing and self-protective measures taken to insure holding onto one's job, even at the price of betraying a co-worker.

We're seeing it in high places in government with prominent figureheads scrambling to cover up their blunders. The Christian work place is not exempt from underhanded tactics either. Talebearing under the guise of "doing what's best for the ministry." Sick, sick approaches to gaining favor. How wearisome and unchristian.

To have your hopes built up then dashed on the rocks of reality is painful. For this woman with the issue of blood, it proved expensive. Your own hopes may have been shattered at some point in time. One older woman had the rug pulled out from under her on more than one occasion by people she respected and trusted. But she said to me, "You know, Rich, those experiences can leave you bitter or better. I chose to let them make me better." She has the scars to prove it.

Your experiences may have left you embittered and distrustful. In the rejection you suffered, you may have been left on the shoals, feeling washed up, barren—the victim of hopes and dreams gone awry. Now you carry with you a lot of private pain and cynicism. You haven't been able to get on with your life and you wallow in anger and self-pity. Oh, the tragedy of a wasted life, for make no mistake you are wasting your life. You may be justified in feeling sorry for yourself. You may have been dealt with unfairly. But to continue in this way is not going to better your situation.

I meet many cynical people. I sense immediately that their cynicism is a coverup for something that happened to them either in the distant past or the more recent present. They've been disillusioned. Some have been kicked around. Abused. If not physically abused, verbally abused. Victimized. Treated unfairly. Pawns in some disgusting event. Wounded. Unappreciated. Never rewarded. Inadequately compensated.

It happens in our churches. I've heard the stories. One incident in their bygone past has shaped their reaction to all that's taking place today. It's stamped them for life. Whom can they trust? Now they find themselves friendless. Who enjoys being around a cynic? Private pain. Rejection of one sort or another. Truly, this is a psychological disturbance of epidemic proportions, infecting the work place, the home, the church, and all of society. Does any of the above describe what you've been through? Are you fearful of risk-taking?

Where Does One Go from Here?

Perhaps something in you longs to break out of this emotional dishevelment. You're truly weary of being torn apart inside. What do you do? How do you break the mold? Will anyone even give you a chance to try to get on with your life, to pick up the pieces, to once again dare to dream, to get back into the mainstream?

Another look at the distressed woman in Mark's gospel account is in order. For 12 years she'd been a tagalong, if she dared to venture out at all. She was hungry for companionship, submerging her restless ambitions. But now she could no longer ignore the silences of her heart. Once she'd had ideals, dreams, aspirations, and feelings of destiny. They were uniquely hers. In her heart of hearts she knew what she was capable of. Nothing could shake her own inner certainties. She was disillusioned, but no wonder. She began to listen to the inner strivings—the voices that would not be silent. And then she'd been hearing reports of this man Jesus. One day she decided to see for herself. What she saw was indelibly impressed upon her mind. The lame walked, the deaf heard, demon-possessed individuals were healed, unclean spirits left the bodies of their victims. To herself she thought, *There's hope for me too!*

When Hope Propels into Action

"She came behind Him in the crowd . . ." Mark says. The result of her touching Him was instantaneous. She knew it. Jesus knew it. When we are cured and healed by natural means—through the skill of physicians, the use of medicines, and the body's defense measures working in our favor—we recover our strength gradually, certainly not all at once.

But as for God, the Bible says, His way is perfect. While it is acknowledged that God heals through medical means as well, when you are miraculously healed you know it. Such was the case with this woman.

It should be noted that when we are delivered from the "disease" of sin, the ill effects of the Adamic curse, we experience a change for the better. Others around us notice. Such are the ways of God.

But hope propelled this woman into action. Did she remember the words of the psalmist? "Why are you cast down, O my soul? And why are you disquieted within me? Hope in God, for I shall yet praise Him for the help of His countenance" (Psalm 42:5).

Whatever the mixed emotions that flooded her being and regardless of her approach—coming from behind so as not to be seen, refusing to risk direct confrontation—she was healed. She came seeking; she left rewarded, blessed, and encouraged.

After one Sunday morning service, I had lunch with a pastor and his family. During the conversation, the pastor said, "Rich, did you happen to notice the woman to your extreme left during your final prayer?" I told him that I had noticed her weeping. That morning at the conclusion of my message I had asked those who were living with a private pain to step into the aisle nearest them and we would pray together for a spiritual release from the problem. She had stepped into the aisle with a hundred others and had talked with the pastor. Nineteen years before, she had an abortion as a teenager. Nobody ever found out. Her husband and three children didn't know. Only the doctor and the woman knew.

She had told the pastor, "That doctor never told me 19 years ago that I would wake up every morning for the rest of my life with the thought in my head going over and over . . . 'You're a baby killer. You murdered your baby.' But, that's exactly what I've heard over and over for 19 years.

"Four years ago our whole family came to faith in Christ. We were truly changed. But, pastor, every day that I've knelt to pray, I've heard the devil say, 'Who do you think you are? You killed your baby. Do you think God will hear the prayer of a woman who's done what you have done?'

"Pastor, for four years I've been able to make just a minimum of progress with the Lord. Every time I try to grow in Christ, the devil brings this brick wall of remembrance into my pathway. I've just about been buried by this private pain.

"This morning after Mr. Wilkerson's message, I decided to give this thing to God, one more time. I looked up into the dome of this old church building to pray. To my amazement I saw Jesus hovering above the crowd. Jesus looked into my eyes.

"I looked into His eyes of compassion. I trembled as I saw Jesus holding my tiny baby in His hands! He said, 'Your baby is with me. Your sin is under the blood. I've forgiven you. You'll see your baby again. Please get on with your life!'

"Pastor, after 19 years it's over. I'm finally free. I don't know why I didn't accept His forgiveness sooner. But, as of this morning it's over, and I'm free!"

Your approach may be timid, yes, even somewhat fearful. You may think that you've railed at God or complained or rebelled too long. Or perhaps you've ignored Him, refusing to acknowledge His existence. Now you think that He won't hear your prayers and see you reach out to Him. It doesn't matter. God understands the reticence, the fear and feelings you've been living with, the rejection you've experienced at the hands of others. These things are known to God. The book of Hebrews tells us that we have a High Priest who sympathizes with our weaknesses (Hebrews 4:15). Therefore, we are told to come boldly to the throne of grace, "that we may obtain mercy and find grace to help in time of need" (v. 16).

Recklessly abandon yourself into the loving hands of the Father. He knows how to catch you. Throw yourself on His mercy. Implore His favor. He is compassionate.

I want you to notice something about Jesus. Why did Jesus know virtue had gone out of Him when the woman touched Him? Did it deplete Him somehow? Did it exhaust Him? No, certainly not, for He has mercy to spare. "For You, Lord, are good, and ready to forgive, and abundant in mercy to all those who call upon You" (Psalm 86:5). The original rendering implies that God is "plenteous in mercy." Another translation says He is "abounding in steadfast love to all who call on Him." He has a limitless supply of forgiveness, mercy, and loving-kindness for those who reach out to Him.

While this woman gained a healing, there was something more that Jesus wanted her to receive. Moreover, there was something that He wanted Jairus, the synagogue ruler, to gain from this. Her witness would encourage Jairus, for Jairus was going home to the greatest of human woes—a dead child. Jesus didn't allow her to sneak off, or become absorbed into the crowd of jostling people. Jesus had done something miraculous for her. Now He expected something from her. He was going to give her an opportunity to feel good about herself—something she surely needed. But more, He was providing a means for her to give witness to her healing in the presence of that vast throng. Amazing the psychology of Jesus!

The Old Testament story of David reveals the cry of his heart: "Do not hide your face from your servant; answer me quickly, for I am in trouble. Come near and rescue me; redeem me because of my foes. You know how I am scorned, disgraced, and shamed; all my enemies are before you. Scorn has broken my heart and has left me helpless; I looked for sympathy, but there was none, for comforters, but I found none" (Psalm 69:17-20 NIV).

David's enemies were very abusive to him, but he knew he had a God who would hear his cause and that it would find acceptance. Psalm 69 is a prophetic psalm. Christ's friends forsook Him while He agonized in the Garden of Gethsemane. Subsequent verses foretell Christ's reproach, suffering, and what happened to Him as He agonized on the cross. We have a sympathizing Savior. Be assured your cries are heard by the One who rescued both the woman on the roadside and David in the caves where he hid. Uncounted others have also sought His help in one way or another.

Ponder this truth: Our heavenly Father knows all about risk. He risked making man—knowing man would turn against Him. He risked loving—knowing He would be hated. He risked giving—knowing He would be robbed. He risked sending His Son—knowing He would be rejected. This woman was not the only one who ever lived with risk and neither are you.

> He was despised and rejected by men, a man of sorrows, and familiar with suffering (Isaiah 53:3 NIV).

> Let us then approach the throne of grace with confidence, so that we may receive mercy and find grace to help us in our time of need (Hebrews 4:16 NIV).

Chapter 4

THE DESPAIR FACTOR:

Release from Hopelessness

Jesus is ever communicating strength; He not only holds up before men a great ideal . . . but He ever touches men [and women] in their paralysis, and makes them powerful in the very places of their need with perfect sufficiency.

—G. Campbell Morgan[1]

On the morning of her death, a godly woman handed her daughter her memorial service wishes. That paper revealed that Psalm 27 (KJV) had seen her through near despair, time after time.

That psalm begins:

The Lord is my light and my salvation; whom shall I fear? the Lord is the strength of my life; of whom shall I be afraid?

And that psalm concludes with these words:

I had fainted, unless I had believed to see the goodness of the Lord in the land of the living. Wait on the Lord: be of good courage, and he shall strengthen thine heart [be strong and let thine heart take courage]: wait, I say on the Lord.

What a beautiful legacy to leave one's daughter! There

wasn't much else this widow could leave. Deprived of the support of her husband at an early age, she was left with three small children. She lived with private pain—all the physical, emotional, psychological, and practical problems that early widowhood could bring. Near despair was often her companion.

I don't know what brought you to the pages of this book, but I do know the reason why I've written it. And I sense that your reasons and my reason are the same. Despair haunts the lives of many. Despair abounds throughout the world—despair brought on by a variety of situational difficulties and interrelationship problems. And I've felt the need to address myself to this real despair factor.

We exist in a world where untold thousands of people have lived to see their youthful hopes and dreams dashed on the rocks of despair. Many things contribute to despair. Despair wraps its chains around the soul. Despair cries, "There is no hope, turn back, give up!" But faith answers, "Look up, take hold, forge on!"

A Big Enough God to Meet Every Need

People say to me, "How can God be interested in me? I'm one among so many. There is a sense of futility at the bigness of the universe, the diversity of needs that have always existed, and the smallness of one's own being as a part of the whole.

God is omnipotent. A big word for a beautiful truth. It means He is all-powerful. There is no limit to His power and His authority.

God is omniscient. Another big word for another profound truth. It means He knows all things. He has infinite knowledge.

God is omnipresent. Another incredibly wonderful word that encompasses us and our present mode of time. It means He can be in all places at the same time.

The dictionary tells us these words are strictly applicable to deity. These words apply to God the Father, to His Son, and to the Holy Spirit.

Now I don't intend for this to be a weighty theological treatise, but I know it's important for you to grasp the reality of God's interest in you and His availability to you. I urge you to accept these truths and hang onto them. Such knowledge will go a long way to relieve your despair.

People question God's omnipotence and His omniscience when they are in the midst of private pain, or when they stand by others who have lost a loved one, or are enduring pain, perhaps brought on by a tragic accident of which they are innocent victims. "Where was God when all this happened?" they question. "If God is so powerful then why doesn't He exercise that power and deal with this kind of evil?"

Well, the fact is we do not have a limited God. The psalmist said it best: "Great is our Lord and mighty in power; his understanding has no limit" (Psalm 147:5 NIV). But God will not impose His will on people nor manipulate them and violate their freedom of choice. Read your Bible. Learn from a man like John who was exiled to the Isle of Patmos. Did he roar at God, accusing Him of an unfair deal in life or saying that he deserved better?

Did John know something we don't know? I think he *understood* what we often fail to grasp: The suffering and struggle that comes to us can be used by God in our lives to make us triumphant over sin's sway. I'm sure John and Paul did not have greater knowledge or revelation than we find in the Word of God; but they accepted what they knew, not always understanding God's purpose and His ways. And they believed in Him and trusted him. George Eliot wrote: "Pain is no evil unless it conquers us." That's worth remembering.

A Consciousness of Need

If Jesus walked through your town or city today, what

would He find? On what and on whom would His eyes
fasten? The human condition today is not unlike those days
when He walked the dusty roads of Galilee. Men and
women from every level of life mixed together in the multitudes that surrounded Him.

Hostile scribes and Pharisees suspiciously watched His
every move. They are similar to the religious leaders of our
day who do not hold to biblical truth.

There were beggars by the wayside, and wealthy men and
women who watched and listened with great interest, if not
some skepticism. In the first instance, the beggars represent the jobless, the homeless, the outcasts from society, the
man or woman struggling with a drug addiction, or the
prostitute on the prowl. In the second instance, the wealthy
represent the people in grey or blue pinstriped suits with
their briefcases, the Yuppies (young, upward-striving
professionals), the Wall Street prognosticators, or the Sili-
con Valley entrepreneurs.

Country folk crowded into Jerusalem and into the vil-
lages where Jesus roamed, anxious to see this One who
performed miraculous healings. There were the hungry
who heard of the miraculous feeding of the multitudes with
just a few loaves of bread and some fish. There were the
learned people deeply interested in Jesus' teachings. All
these people rubbed shoulders in the crowds that attended
Jesus wherever He went. And were He to traverse in our
midst today, He'd find the same mixed multitude. Would
He find you?

The answer to that is yes. If you were there, He would
know it. If your need was of such urgency that you wormed
your way through that jostling crowd (like the woman who
was in such desperate straits), Jesus would recognize your
presence. How? Why? *Because Jesus always knows the difference between the jostle of a curious mob and the touch of a soul in
agony and despair.*

Private pain never goes unnoticed by the Master.

After one Sunday evening service, a man came to the stage and said, "Mr. Wilkerson, I have a young friend who feels like the world has forgotten him. He was a star football player on the state championship football team.

"This past September, in the middle of the season, he was driving home with friends one night after a party. They had all been drinking. He lost control of the car and crashed into a tree.

"Everyone walked away from the accident except the football star. The steering wheel broke and literally pushed into his head. He was in a coma until the end of November. His motor capabilities will eventually come back entirely if he works hard. But he has lost his will to work.

"His former friends want nothing to do with him. I felt compelled to talk to you."

I looked at the man and said, "Bring him to my room on Tuesday."

Tuesday afternoon, the gentleman showed up with the young man, the former football star. His gait was slow and it was easy to see that everything was not all right.

The young man haltingly told me that he had a deep pain in his heart, pain that just wouldn't go away. He raised the sleeve of his shirt; stitch marks told the story of four different suicide attempts.

I can't explain what happened next, but faith flooded my soul. As I spoke to that young man my faith began to lift his despair. A gleam appeared in his eyes.

I said, "I want you to go home this afternoon and consider what I've said. If you truly believe that God can take you past this problem to real victory, then I want you to come back and hear me talk tonight.

"If you decide to come back, I want you to bring a 'No-Suicide Contract' with you. You write it out on a piece of paper and say, *With God's help, I'll never try to take my life again, but rather I will give my life wholeheartedly to Christ.*"

We prayed and they left. That night the auditorium was packed. When I gave the call for people who wanted to come to faith in Christ, the aisles quickly filled with those in need of forgiveness. As the people made their way down the aisles, I noticed to my right the same young man being helped to the altar. His right hand was raised, waving the No-Suicide Contract.

Jesus picked him out of the crowd, saw his need, and changed his life. That's the Jesus I'm telling you about.

The people Jesus brought into prominence and immortalized in the Bible were all of one class—they were needy people. Not only was Jesus a great Teacher, but He drew to Himself those who were troubled, despairing—those who needed His look of love and His touch. They were drawn to Him as surely as iron is drawn to a magnet.

The needy who turned to Him never left disappointed. In many instances, He turned to the needy, those who were powerless to come to Him, and lifted them from their despair. There was so much power in Him that weakness felt its attraction.

Consciousness of their own need drove them to Him. Jesus rendered need conspicuous so that He might meet it and cancel it. Such is still the power of our heavenly advocate today. You can be the beneficiary of that power. The tragedy is that so few know that Jesus is within reach.

G. Campbell Morgan, the great expositor, teacher, preacher, and writer of a previous generation, points out how people are drawn out of the crowds, one by one, and brought into living contact with Christ. Christ deals with them not impersonally, but on an individual basis. "He is ever communicating strength. . . . He ever touches men in their paralysis, and makes them powerful in the very places of their need with perfect sufficiency."[2]

An Eclipse in the Soul

In the twin accounts of despair recorded by three of the

Gospel writers (see Matthew 9:18-26; Mark 5:21-43; and Luke 8:40-56), we encounter the agonized entreaty of a father whose daughter lay dying. Jairus' whole existence was threatened by the shadowy specter of death. What was this man's need? What drew him to Jesus? Jairus was driven by his sense of impending sorrow.

Perhaps you are already in the throes of sorrow. You are feeling that it is too late. Death has already done its awful work. Your despair is devastating. Jesus sees your broken heart. Your sorrow is not being ignored. He is always sensitive to human sorrow and tragedy. Look again at Jesus as He responds to Jairus. There is tenderness and strength in Jesus' attitude and in His actions, and the result is peace and joy in place of turmoil and sorrow.

"But Jesus hasn't given me back my daughter (son, wife, husband . . . the loved one you've lost)," you protest. "How can you say I can experience peace and joy when my heart is breaking?"

What can one realistically expect? Can you expect complete deliverance from this very real pain? The answer to that is *no* and *yes*. *No* to the word *complete*, and *yes* to the word *deliverance*.

Perhaps you are thinking, *What kind of an answer is that!* I'll tell you. Do you want to be completely free of the sense of loss that you are experiencing because this loved one is no longer around? Of course, you don't want to be free of the memories of this dear one. There will always be a sense of loss that you will rightfully experience because you loved this person. You will preserve and cherish the memories and even come to value the lessons this pain taught you. But the pain does diminish. Pain is a powerful teacher, but one of the wisest teachers you will ever have.

Pain never leaves us where we were. If we are willing to allow the pain to teach us, we move on to become stronger, wiser, more compassionate, more understanding, more loving. Pain can bring a wealth of good things into our lives to deliver us from that awful loneliness and bereavement. In time—and that is a key—we come to regard the loss in a different light. God is providentially at work in our lives; He knows what we need to mold us into His pattern for us. We have hidden resources that even we didn't know we possessed. God is refining us, difficult as this may be to accept. But it can and will happen if we allow it. Time doesn't heal; God does. But He uses the seemingly slow process of time to effect long-lasting healing. In place of the pain will come courage to face our circumstances honestly, the wisdom to understand what God wants us to do, and the strength to do it. On top of that, in response to our turning to Him in prayer, He will provide the faith to be patient while He works out His perfect will for our lives.

For now, perhaps the pain of the death of a loved one is too fresh and real for you to be open to answers. You may not even appreciate the reference to Bible verses. But I am not there to put my arms around you and to comfort you, so let these words fall on your heart now. And then come back to this later when you may be more receptive to what God has to say to you in His Word. "Rest [trust] in the Lord, and wait patiently for Him" (Psalm 37:7).

When we come back to the account of Jesus and Jairus, we see how it was impossible for Jesus to move easily. The people crowded Him. It wasn't intentional rudeness, but simply their longing to be near Him. The people were curious, to be sure, but they weren't unsympathetic to the needs of others. But what they didn't comprehend was Jesus' capacity for love and His ability to lavish that love on all who needed it. He waited for the opportunity—their willingness to come to Him to receive what they needed.

So it is for you. To receive, you must be willing to draw near, to open yourself to what He is prepared to give. He would pour into your heart the healing balm of His comfort and strength, His resources to meet your despair. "Answer me quickly, O Lord; my spirit faints with longing"

(Psalm 143:7 NIV), David cried. Let it be your cry. Let me point you in the direction of these psalms. There is help and hope for you within the pages of God's Word. The Word is God speaking. We deprive ourselves of that which can sustain us through the eclipses of our soul when we fail to reach for His touch.

What is needed is self-disclosure—a relinquishing of our hold on the private pain so that God can do His work of healing. We need to ventilate our neurotic, throbbing emotions. We have to put ourselves in the posture of trusting His greatness and understanding. His omnipotence is no barrier to His moving upon the human scene today with power to touch us in our despair.

Paul Tournier, eminent Swiss theologian, explains that man's basic loneliness is linked with fear. We fear one another, fear being crushed in life, fear being misunderstood, fear another disappointment. "Thus fear breeds loneliness and conflict; loneliness and conflict breed fear. To heal the world, we must give men an answer to fear and restore among them the sense of community," Tournier points out.[3] As long as we shrink back in fear, we will not experience release from despair and depression.

A Dead Girl and a Sick Woman

Jairus may have felt fear and panic when Jesus suddenly stopped, turned around, looked over the crowd, and asked, "Who touched My clothes?"

At that moment, while not unaware of the mission He was on, Jesus' thoughts were directed not to a dead child (for she was already dead), but to a living woman. Please understand, I do not mean this to sound unkind: Jesus is not touched with pity for those who die who know Him. Jesus knows what awaits the believer in the glories of heaven; the Father has prepared for their arrival the moment they step across that threshhold marked death. In death, the innocent little girl was safe and Jesus knew it. But it was needful for Jesus to take time to minister to the living.

Jesus paused as much for Jairus' sake as for the woman's. He was going to lead Jairus into an atmosphere that would increase his faith. Shortly, they would be walking into Jairius' home where there was much weeping, wailing, and confusion. If I had been Jairus, I'm almost sure I'd have been impatient, thinking, *Someone is hindering Jesus from making haste to get to my daughter*. Jairus was our predecessor in this experience of feeling anxiety, grief, and pain.

The Clutch of the Hand of Despair

Deep as was the sorrow of Jairus, the diseased woman's sorrow was grievous too. Despair was her companion. How she managed to work her way through that crowd remains a mystery. Have you ever tried to work your way through a crowd, perhaps a crowd making its way into Disneyland or a ballpark? It is difficult for those of us who are in good health and full of vim and vigor to make our way through the mall at Christmastime. So think of the woman—weak and wan, worn and emaciated, yet she reached Jesus!

The word "touched" doesn't convey the true meaning of what this woman did. We get nearer to the meaning of the Greek verb when we recognize that she clutched Him. She grasped something. What was it? She fastened upon the *kraspedon*, the tassel in the corner of His garment (see Numbers 15:37-41). This was an Eastern garment worn by Jesus in keeping with the ritual and commandment of the Old Testament. Hers was a daring and desperate venture. The law said she was not to touch, but in her agony and helplessness, her strength ebbing away, she thought to herself, *If I can make contact with this man, I shall get help*. It was the clutch of the hand of despair.

The woman didn't understand about faith, yet she possessed enough to act upon it. There are those who believe she acted somewhat out of superstition. In the book of Acts, we have reference to those who came to the apostle Paul with their handkerchiefs so that he could anoint them; the people carried these back to loved ones who received miracle healings. God honored this at that time (see Acts 19:11,12). These, too, were desperate acts—faith expressing itself albeit somewhat superstitiously. But they were healed. And so was this woman. And what did God do? He ignored the superstition; He honored the little bit of faith. "Daughter, your faith [that is, your trust and confidence in Me, springing from faith in God] has restored you to health. Go in [to] peace, and be continually healed and free from your [distressing bodily] disease" (Mark 5:34 AMP).

And I tell you this to encourage you. You are despairing. You sense in yourself a lack of faith. This makes you fearful. Or perhaps at one time you possessed great faith, but something occurred that brought you into despair and you have remained there. Your situation hasn't changed. Now you doubt more than believe. Notice once again Jesus' words to this woman. It was her faith, not her superstition. It was her contact with Jesus. It wasn't perfect faith, rather it was imperfect and even limited in scope. But it was sincere.

God doesn't wait until we reach a state of perfection in our belief. When we feel our hopelessness and come to Him for help, He never withholds that help. There may still be a lot of fear when we initially reach for Him, but He understands our previous disillusionment. And so it was that Jesus perceived the touch of this woman's trembling fingers as she clutched that tassel. As small as your faith may be, Jesus would have you act on it. The promise is not universal, i.e., that physical healing comes to all; but there are resources available to see you through your despair. The greater healing for this woman was beyond the physical, as important and needful as that was. She was released from the bondage of despair. Peace was the greater gift.

Ponder this truth: Like all who openly confess Christ, the woman found a new awareness and assurance of His saving power. And she found an inner peace that released her from the stranglehold of despair. "Thou wilt keep him in perfect peace, whose mind is stayed on thee: because he trusteth in thee" (Isaiah 26:3 KJV).

David prayed this prayer when he was in hiding in a cave: "When my spirit grows faint within me, it is you who know my way. In the path where I walk men have hidden a snare for me. Look to my right and see; no one is concerned for me. I have no refuge; no one cares for my life" (Psalm 142:3,4 NIV). That is utter despair. But notice the remaining words of that prayer: "I cry to you, O Lord; I say, 'You are my refuge, my portion in the land of the living.' Listen to my cry, for I am in desperate need; rescue me from those who pursue me, for they are too strong for me. Set me free from my prison that I may praise your name. Then the righteous will gather about me because of your goodness to me" (vv. 5-7 NIV).

Whatever your prison of despair, the Father is waiting to free you.

> When obstacles and trials seem
> Like prison walls to be,
> I do the little I can do
> And leave the rest to Thee.
>
> And when there seems no chance, no change,
> From grief can set me free,
> Hope finds its strength in helplessness,
> And calmly waits for Thee.
> —Author Unknown

Chapter 5

THE BONDAGE FACTOR:

Captive to an Enslaving Addiction

God whispers to us in our pleasures, speaks in our conscience, but shouts in our pains: it is His megaphone to rouse a deaf world.

—C. S. Lewis[1]

Not all chains are made of iron. There are lifestyle habits we impose upon ourselves that shackle us and hold us captive. The message of this chapter is a liberating one. You can break out. Do you want to break away from your bondage? All you have to lose is your chains. What you stand to gain is freedom from the private pain of bondage.

Bondage. It's a hard word. A word that brings to mind slavery. The dictionary defines bondage as *subjection to some force, compulsion, or influence.* Captivity. Shackles. Chains. What does the word conjure up in your thinking?

In what way is bondage a form of private pain? When you are captive to an enslaving addiction, for instance, and you fear being found out, that's private pain. It could be alcoholism, drugs, cigarettes, gluttony, pornography, or some other kind of secret problem. Such bondage brings fear upon its victims. Fear and shame. When you don't want someone to know about your problem, you dread the possibility of discovery.

Such bondage exists, of course, even when one's addiction is known and you can't shake the habit. But it's still a form of private pain because, deep down, if you are perfectly honest, you want to be free of the compulsive habit. We are talking about emotional disorder brought on because of conflict between one's behavior and values. This leads to intense despair and feelings of hopelessness which, in turn, can send the individual back to his addictive habit as a means of escape. It becomes a vicious cycle. There is loneliness and guilt compounding the problem.

Those who live with alcoholics, for instance, would tell you there is always evasion of blame and defensiveness. This propensity to evade responsibility for one's own destructive behavior can be traced back to the dawn of time—Adam blamed God for giving him "the woman [who] gave me to eat," and Eve blamed the serpent who "beguiled" her. Self-deceit. This kind of behavior in the alcoholic or chemically dependent person finally becomes pathological, the result of deep disturbances caused by the disease.

Such private pain exacts a terrible toll in relationships that wane and wither and eventually there may come total estrangement. It can produce spiritual deterioration and lead to total spiritual collapse.

Bondage can lead to suicidal moods and even to the culmination of the suicide act. Some suicides are not necessarily overt, that is, the individual may commit slow suicide through continued use of drugs, refusal to seek help in overcoming his alcohol problem, or continuation of smoking.

The publisher of *The Saturday Evening Post* tells of going into a hospital and seeing men dying of emphysema, yet with their dying breaths puffing on cigarettes. A nurse in a veteran's hospital speaks of cancer victims agonizing in their last days, yet begging for a cigarette.

A 35-year-old, the father of four young children, had emergency triple-bypass heart surgery. Yet he went back to smoking shortly after his return home. His wife also had a health problem and was told that smoking was one of the worst things she could do; yet she clung to her addiction.

Men and women in bondage to addicting habits.

Or consider the plight of the person who is a slave to the bottle. I think of my friends who discovered that their son was an alcoholic. What heartache those parents endured! And what anguish this man brought upon himself, his wife, and children. Happily, in this instance, the family came to his rescue and he responded and received help from Alcoholics Anonymous.

But that doesn't always happen. I heard of an alcoholic woman whose husband left her because of her drinking. Now she has dragged her 16-year-old son into the same wretched lifestyle. Her lovely Christian mother grieves over this only child and grandchild. How many men, women, and young people are caught in the grip of addiction?

And what are we to say of the widespread use of other drugs in our society today! A woman told me about driving to work at 7:45 one morning. When she stopped at a stoplight in front of a high school she watched a stoop-shouldered young person, shuffling along, holding a Coke in one hand. He walked a few feet, head down, turned, walked back, and repeated his steps six times; then he stopped, walked in a circle, and finally repeated the previous strange walking pattern. In between, he would gulp on his Coke. One block further down the road, she saw the same kind of strange behavior from another adolescent with a Mohawk punk haircut and weird-looking attire. Undoubtedly, these two teenagers were strung out on drugs on their way to school.

I think of the closet-drinkers. Women who are caught in the clutches of alcoholism and drugs who seek escape from their private pain. Men who can't get through the pressure-cooker atmosphere that surrounds them at work unless they have their midday drinks. People who come home and reach for their after-work drink to "unwind." Individuals who drink themselves into oblivion, day after day. The derelicts of society—both men and women—who can't afford the Betty Ford treatment like the upper strata of society are often abandoned by their families. They walk the streets, clutching their brown sack, unshaven, unkempt, homeless winos in captivity to an uncontrolled habit.

We live in a culture that is characterized by stress. Whatever the stressful cause, people are copping out rather than seeking solutions or learning how to cope.

Alcoholism becomes a sickness, a disease, a total chemical dependency. Its victims need care and counseling. Smoking is considered to be the most pervasive addiction of all, just as real as drug addiction. The alcoholic turns to his security bottle; the smoker to that slender white weed he can hold onto between his fingers. The drug addict gulps the pill, snorts the powder, or shoots the fix—anything to blot out the pain that accompanies stressful living.

I believe that freedom from the private pain of such bondage will not come until the individual desires freedom more than bondage. Some people learn to live with their chains. They make excuses and allowances for them. They make plans around their private pain. They rationalize. Sometimes they will enlist the help of the few people around them who know of their enslaving habits. They promise themselves (and loved ones who know) that tomorrow they'll change; tomorrow they'll quit. The agony and guilt they endure and the helplessness they feel can scarcely be imagined by those of us who haven't experienced their private pain.

Besetting Sins

Satan has many well-laid traps that ensnare God's people. We are not exempt from the slavery of besetting sins. I meet many people who wrestle with certain habits that have become a part of their lives. They get victory for awhile; then they are plunged back into their bondage by circumstances. Once again, they find themselves in chains. Their confessions are heartrending.

If this describes you, I understand what you are going through. Your humiliating defeat at the hands of the enemy is well-known to me. You've been robbed of spiritual vitality, time after time. Your secret sin has caused you untold hours of private shame and pain. Many well-meaning Christians continue to fall victim to besetting sins; and guilt, condemnation, worry, anxiety, loneliness, emptiness, and despair are their daily companions.

Prodigals in Bondage

Even the biblical "prodigal son," as public as his story is, was overwhelmed by private pain. Certainly this son wasn't ready to broadcast to the world that he had squandered his inheritance on "riotous living" and was now residing in a pigpen.

What was his problem? The Bible says he "squandered his wealth in wild living" (Luke 15:13 NIV). Wild living. Drinking? Drugs? Wine, women, and song? Obviously some form of gross waywardness. Willful choice on the part of this young son. Self-indulgence. The results are sketched in appalling colors: disillusionment, suffering, slavery, and despair.

Vernon E. Johnson, founder and president emeritus of the Johnson Institute in Minneapolis (which deals with alcoholism), points out that virtually all the basic spiritual dynamics of alcoholism are present in the events and relationships of the prodigal's story. Alcohol is first used to add zest to life. It is in no sense considered an experiment with evil but rather, with what is essentially *good*. It's what "the beautiful people" do, right? Johnson shows that the goal is to enhance life—to give it more zing.

Johnson says it can be likened to today's younger son going to Las Vegas and slipping into one pleasure palace after another:

On down what seems like a never-ending street he

goes, pursuing his rainbows to the end of the line. Finally, his resources are thoroughly wasted (another word so descriptive of alcoholism). It is in the pit of self-degradation that the turning point comes for the young man in the parable. The physical description of his environment could not be more devastating. He has been sent to feed swine. . . . In the same fashion, the chemically dependent person chases the rainbows of euphoria, seemingly heedless of the rising costs to himself and others. . . . In the end, if it is allowed to progress that far, all resources are spent: health, wealth, feelings of self-worth, and all dear relationships. All he once had is laid waste; all he once was is gone. There is nothing left now but to crawl away and die.[2]

Jay Strack, in his book *Drugs and Drinking: The All American Cop-Out*, points out that the great "turn-on" among millions of teenagers today can be attributed to several factors. Using the acrostic "peace," he focuses on the most important reasons for drug-taking given by teens across the country:

P ressure
E scape
A vailability
C uriosity
E mptiness

One, or a combination, or all of these factors may have prompted the biblical prodigal to ask for his inheritance and take off from home. The human condition hasn't changed through the centuries.

The Inevitable Consequences of Sin

The young prodigal's extravagances led to misery, an

inevitable consequence of going astray. His "give me" attitude as he confronted his father, demanding his fortune, revealed his selfishness. Present gratification was a consuming passion; he wanted his liberty and money so he could go on his merry way. But, as the prodigal learned, liberty to sin is slavery. The folly of his ways would rise up to haunt him and he would have plenty of time to reflect in private pain.

I have encountered scores of young people flaunting independence and experiencing disillusionment and early burnout. These individuals have all but ruined themselves by their foolish ambition to be independent. They are just kids who have resented parental restraints—restraints that were meant for their own good.

I have met adults, too, shackled by pride and an unwillingness to admit that somewhere along the line they made a mistake or mistakes. Now they hide behind a facade, in bondage to self. But make no mistake, they are living in pain.

I have an acquaintance who was raised to fear and respect the living God. At one time he was a minister of the gospel, but he left the ministry for the business world.

God blessed him with a wonderful wife and family. He had it all! But hidden underneath was the lust of the flesh. He yielded to this private sin and began to step out on his wife. All along he continued to play the part of Mr. Christian. Behind the scenes, he was becoming very abusive toward his wife.

Alcohol became a part of his life. Gambling was next. One thing led to another until he lost everything he had worked so hard to gain. His children want nothing to do with him. His grandchildren are not allowed to visit him.

Pride keeps this man from yielding to God. His pride has robbed him of the abundant life Christ came to give. He's traded it all for a lie.

Several things can be noted about private pain that results from being captive to an enslaving habit, or an addiction to pornography, or even gluttony. It could even be the opposite of overeating—anorexia—or you may be in bondage to painful memories.

Bondage can take many forms. Usually bondage:

1. Represents a state of departure and distance from God.
2. Is a spending state; a terrible waste of one's life, not to mention one's resources (financial), and one's health.
3. Is a wanting state. The old saying "willful waste brings woeful want" is true. An individual in bondage throws away the mercy and help of God and ignores the voice of his conscience, the "still small voice of God." In many instances, the very necessities of life are wasted and he ends up in poverty.
4. Is a sinful state that results in servitude, a condition the Bible describes as being a "servant of sin" (see John 8:34 KJV). It's a sense of deep loss of things once held dear and meaningful: virtue, honor, respect from family and friends, and supremely, estrangement from God—of being off in "the far country" like the prodigal.
5. Is a condition of perpetual dissatisfaction. Once recognition of his bondage comes upon the individual, down deep he senses shame, loss of self-respect, grief, just a total dissatisfied feeling that cannot be comforted.
6. Is a pitiful condition of madness and frenzy; a final realization that unless he changes, there is no hope.

There Is a Living Hope

I have painted a bleak picture. I do not intend to leave it

there. Yet, you cannot portray private pain that is linked to enslaving habits as anything other than dark and miserable. But for the Christian, life in Christ offers a living hope. And that is always what God offers. We see this in the parable of the prodigal son where the grace of God softens the hardest heart. The fatherhood of God is portrayed in the father of this wayward son, offering a touching picture of despair conquered by hope when the son returns to his father.

I do not intend to give you simplistic advice or pious sermons as a Band-Aid approach to an enormous problem. The bondage of private pain is endemic across the country. I believe in God's miracle-working power, and I invite you to ask God for a miracle for your condition. You need a miracle as much as the hemorrhagic woman needed one. God healed her instantly. But the miracle for both this woman and the prodigal son began when they decided to do something.

I think the lesson is clear. There must be more than a "want to," there must be a willingness "to do" something. The prodigal son said, "I will set out and go back to my father and say to him: Father, I have sinned against heaven and against you. I am no longer worthy to be called your son. . . . So he got up and went to his father" (Luke 15:18-20 NIV). This was the wayward son's decision and it was the first step on his road to recovery.

Notice he said, "I will." He was taking charge of that private pain. He was saying, "I am no longer going to live like this. I'm not going to accept this bondage any longer. This is one private pain I can do something about."

But the prodigal didn't anticipate what he got from his father. At best, he expected his father to allow him to be one of the hired servants. But that didn't happen—he was the father's son. The father was going to help the son to accept himself as he was. Wisely enough he would not allow his son to evade what the son unconsciously wanted to evade—acceptance of himself and his problem. The father's forgiveness opened the door for healing and restoration—a release from the prodigal's private pain.

Recovery and Release from Bondage Is Possible

There is a way for you or your loved ones to be freed too. Spiritual and emotional recovery is possible—difficult, yes, requiring gut-level surrender! But wholeness, deliverance, release, and freedom from bondage can result. In the account of the prodigal son we see the son *coming* to himself, *admitting* to his own degradation, *turning* from it, *returning* to his father, *confessing* his fault and folly, and *pleading* for the father's mercy and help. And what happened? His father received him with respect. He came home in rags; his father adorned him. He came home hungry; his father not only fed him, but feasted him. Remember, such is the way of the Father-heart of God. He is waiting to receive prodigals—to release them from their prison of private pain. Hold in your mind's eye this picture of God as your heavenly Father—waiting, longing to receive and help you. But the first step is the one you take in the direction of God, ready to confess and forsake that which is holding you in bondage.

Pay attention to the megaphone of pain through which God is shouting in your ear. Sometimes His voice is quiet, at other times He is altogether silent. But in situations like this, I rather think He is shouting to get your attention even as C. S. Lewis suggests:

> God whispers to us in our pleasures,
> speaks in our conscience,
> but shouts in our pains;
> it is his megaphone to rouse a deaf world.

Mr. Lewis wrote:

> No doubt pain as God's megaphone is a terrible instrument . . . [but] it plants the flag of truth within the fortress of a rebel soul. . . . If God were proud He would hardly have us . . . but He is not proud, He stoops to conquer.[3]

Allow yourself to be so conquered; I can assure you, your private pain will be vanquished.

Hands-on Management

In the book *You Never Stop Being a Parent*, Helen Hosier has a chapter entitled "Hands-on Management" in which she talks about addictive habits that can keep an individual in bondage. Helen sent out 500 questionnaires and compiled the responses of parents of adult children. In addition, she interviewed many parents personally. What she learned makes for enlightening reading. She says, "There's more to alcoholism than a hangover . . . alcohol is the most overused drug on the market." Parents with adult children who are alcoholics or enslaved by other addictive habits, should urge their children to seek God's help, as well as any means available for detoxification. These are important steps on the path to seeking permanent release from bondage.

There is much misunderstanding about the role of psychology and recognized educational programs and organizations that have good track records. Christians often say, "But God doesn't need help." This spiritual naiveté is disturbing and contributes to much of their own private pain. They close their minds to ideas that come from sources other than the Bible. That kind of a mindset fails to understand that all truth is God's truth; if something has proven workable and true, it has God's stamp of approval.

Thus we see many parents locked into a sick relationship with chemically dependent children. Or we see adult victims of a chemical dependency in bondage to their addiction or enslaving habit, whatever it might be. Obviously, more is needed than what Andre Bustanoby calls "a spiritual fix." It is time for us to remove our blinders and come to grips with reality. No one can accuse Rich Wilkerson of not believing in spiritual solutions. Of course, I am devoted to Bible reading and study, to the practical application of biblical truth into my life and the lives of those with whom I come in contact. I believe in prayer and fasting and in whatever spiritual exercise is necessary to release a problem into the hands of God. But I am also all for personal responsibility, and the need to become informed and then acting intelligently. Once again, I point you to the biblical example of the prodigal son and the hemorrhagic woman; both of them did something about their problems. We need to behave responsibly when facing problems, even when Scripture does not give specific solutions.

"While helping people who are in bondage is difficult, it is not impossible. A key word, for instance, in alcoholism is *denial*," Helen Hosier points out. She's right. I've seen it time after time. It's not easy to confront our weaknesses and what the Bible calls "the sin that so easily besets us."

> Some dynamic new approaches are proving to be quite successful in helping the victims of the destructive disease, alcoholism. One such program, founded by Vernon E. Johnson, D.D. [already mentioned], of the Johnson Institute, a nonprofit foundation in Minneapolis, Minnesota, trains family members to be "interveners." . . . Results have been astounding. Eight times out of ten, family members are successful in achieving their goal—the victim perceives and accepts the severity of his illness and agrees to enter a treatment program. This is called educated early intervention—and the first crucial step is to make a willing patient out of a victim.[4]

Caring Confrontation

Caring confrontation is another word for hands-on management. Those in bondage need help and a program whereby they can experience the rebirth for which they unknowingly thirst. They need the kind of supportive help that comes across as being noncondemning. The church can help provide this.

There are those who question whether addiction is a sin or a sickness. Dr. Gary Collins in his book *Christian Counseling* answers this to my satisfaction:

> The addict originally chose to subject his or her body to a poison, but the poison then took control and the person became powerless to stop the deterioration without help from others. Addicts and their families are not helped by moralizing about the sins of drug abuse; neither is it fair to dismiss drug abuse as a sickness, devoid of wrongdoing and for which there is no responsibility. The addict must be helped professionally to overcome the sickness and taught spiritually to live the rest of his life in obedience and submission to Jesus Christ. Only then is the difficult problem truly and effectively resolved.[5]

The Tyranny of Nicotine

John Powell once struggled with "the tyranny of nicotine" as he describes it. In trying to give up the habit, he experienced "brief little victories." He explains:

> But there was always that weak moment when I promised myself it would be "just one," and I was back in my old chains, a prisoner of my old habits. When medical evidence began to pile up, and lung cancer, heart trouble, emphysema, and respiratory infections were linked rather conclusively to my tyrant, I tried again and again, but in the end my efforts were always unsuccessful. More and more I felt helpless and conquered, and this is for me—with my well cultivated myth of self-sufficiency and strength—the most difficult of all admissions. On an even deeper level I had strong guilt feelings about my weakness.[6]

To hear this great man of God admit to such human fallibility will be, I believe, an encouragement to the reader. That he experienced much private pain over his addiction is clearly evident. He continues:

> One morning, while I was praying and dying to get to that first cup of coffee and cigarette, I had the feeling that God wanted me to talk to Him about this matter. So I admitted my shame to Him, and I remember ending with the painful admission that "I guess I just don't have the strength." Figuratively I threw myself at His feet and crumbled there under the weight of my repeated failures at self-conquest.
>
> Then I heard the words inside me: *I have the strength for you. It is yours if you ask for it.*
>
> "Okay," I said, "You give me Your strength and You've got Yourself a deal."
>
> All I can tell you is that since that moment several years ago I have not smoked. As I remember, there were the so-called "nicotine fits" for a very short while, and then all inclination to smoke disappeared completely. What is even more mysterious to me is that God seems to have erased all memory of what it was like to smoke. . . . I feel like a person who has never smoked. I think my present attitudes and freedom are comparable to those of the many members of Alcoholics Anonymous who know that they have won sobriety only through the strength of a power greater than themselves, only through the strength of God infused into them.[7]

Ponder this truth: John Powell explains that the knowledge that God really wanted to be intimately close to him was a turning point in his relationship with the Father. "I needed to be rid of the deistic concept of God as distant, uninterested, inoperative in me. . . . I needed to feel the touch of God. . . ."[8]

What John Powell accepted, and what many others have learned, is that God didn't turn His back on him because of his bondage. He loved John in spite of his sins. God's anger against sin is always balanced by His great love and pity for His suffering children.

My cousin David Wilkerson says, "While we sinners are swimming against the tide, God is always on shore ready to throw us a lifeline." David says sin is like an octopus with many tentacles trying to crush out our lives. He also makes the analogy of being in hand-to-hand combat as we fight in a personal war with the enemy. God wants to be our Commander, and He dispatches the Holy Spirit to us with clear directions on how to fight, when to run, and where to strike next. It's important to understand that this battle we are fighting is war against the devil and we have to be volunteers in the fight. Our part in this battle is to believe that God will bring us victoriously through the battle.

In the book of Hebrews we are told to lay aside the weight, the sin which does so easily beset us, surrounding and harassing us, and "to run with patient endurance and steady and active persistence the appointed course of the race that is set before us, looking away [from all that will distract] to Jesus, Who is the Leader and the Source of our faith" (see Hebrews 12:1,2 AMP).

The apostle Paul wrote much about coming out from under the slavery of sin to being a slave of God (see Romans 6). This happens when we are set free from our self-imposed bondage (in whatever form that may be). Paul describes the enslaving weakness of the flesh, but he also describes the power in being "more than conquerors through him who loved us" (Romans 8:37).

Whether it is through the help and administration of an organized program, or a caring confrontation by one's family or friends, or a miracle of immediate deliverance from the Lord, it is the touch of God that frees us from bondage and sets us into the glorious freedom of being a child of God (see Romans 8:21). That touch is an ever-gentle touch, "like a soft hand caressing the face of [the] soul."

God uses various means to touch the seeking soul. I urge you to submit to His touch, and when you do, the promise is that no future temptation can ever overtake you because God is faithful. He will not allow you to be tempted beyond what you are able to take—with the temptation He will make a way of escape, so you can bear it and stand up under it (see 1 Corinthians 10:13).

The apostle Peter testified that God knows how to deliver the godly out of temptations (2 Peter 2:9).

We have the testimony of John the Revelator, "the beloved disciple," that "if anyone sins, we have an Advocate with the Father, Jesus Christ the righteous" (1 John 2:1). And that "Greater is he that is in you, than he that is in the world" (1 John 4:4 KJV).

God has provided weapons for this warfare, and He is not nearly as grieved by our yielding to temptation as He is by our not learning how to deal with it. It is what we do not do that hurts the Father. Therefore, to maintain spiritual vigor, it is vital that we learn to use these weapons. With these weapons we can conquer fear—the fear of Satan's power. Remember, God doesn't give the spirit of fear—that is one of the enemy's weapons. Hear what the apostle Paul said about this:

> For though we live in the world, we do not wage war as the world does. The weapons we fight with are not the weapons of the world. On the contrary, they have divine power to demolish strongholds. We demolish arguments and every pretension that sets itself up against the knowledge of God, and we take captive every thought to make it obedient to Christ (2 Corinthians 10:3-5 NIV).

John Baillie wrote that the New Testament does not say

"You shall know the rules and by them you shall be bound," but "You shall know the truth, and the truth shall make you free" (John 8:32).

> Fearing to launch on "full surrender's" tide,
> I asked the Lord where would its waters glide.
> My little bark, "To troubled seas I dread?"
> "Unto Myself," He said.
>
> Unto Himself! No earthly tongue can tell
> The bliss I find, since in His heart I dwell;
> The things that charmed me once seem all as
>   naught;
> Unto Himself I'm brought.
> —Author Unknown

Chapter 6

THE GUILT FACTOR:

Guilt with a Capital G

> Almost certainly the greatest problem plagu-
> ing mankind is guilt and shame. Its influence is
> widespread and its effects on all of our lives is
> staggering.
>
> —Dwight L. Carlson, M.D.[1]

"Guilt, guilt, guilt! It's all around us—it's everywhere,"
so writes Dwight L. Carlson, M.D., who claims all of us
wrestle with guilt in some way almost every day.

Students feel guilt about cheating on tests, smoking pot,
or going too far with the opposite sex. Other individuals
experience guilt about exaggerating on their income tax,
cheating on their mates, padding expense accounts, or telling "white lies" to get them off the hook or to cover why they
skipped church or couldn't go to someone's party.

It seems we're always making excuses or being defensive.
People put us on the spot. Demands are made upon our
time. We feel guilty when we don't accept an invitation or do
something that's expected of us. Businessmen and women
express guilt because of the long hours they put in on the
job.

We apologize and feel guilty when we buy ourselves a new
item of clothing, get a different car, or redecorate our
house—especially when we hear comments about what
we've done. However, we're not above putting others on a
guilt trip when we have the opportunity. We don't mean to

inflict guilt, but it happens because we are all so prone to feeling guilty.

Feeling guilty is a way of life for many. We spend an inordinate amount of time and energy regretting things we've said or done. Guilt. It's so pervasive. And it causes a tremendous amount of private pain.

The Origin of Guilt

In the biblical account of Adam and Eve in the Garden of Eden, we read that they succumbed to the wiles of the serpent and did not resist the temptation of the devil. They fell. This is referred to as original sin.

It is the first recorded instance of guilt because immediately the eyes of Adam and Eve were opened; they tried to cover their nakedness. Guilt does that—we seek ways to cover up, we make excuses, we try to get rid of those uncomfortable feelings that guilt produces. As a result of Adam and Eve's sin, God pronounced the death sentence on all mankind (Romans 5:12-21).

But He is a gracious God, loving and long-suffering. He didn't leave mankind without a way of escape nor without hope. God provided His Son, Christ, the sinless One, to take the sentence of death for us (1 Peter 3:18).

We must appropriate what God through Christ has already done for us. We deal with our guilt and basic alienation from the Father by accepting His Son into our lives: "For God so loved the world that He gave His only begotten Son, that whoever believes in Him should not perish but have everlasting life" (John 3:16).

Until we come to grips with original sin and its hold on us, we are guilty before a righteous God. So the first thing we need to do is to make certain we stand in right relationship with the Father through Christ. "For all have sinned and fall short of the glory of God" (Romans 3:23).

Some of you may intellectually assent to all of this. You've heard it a hundred times or more. You go to church Sunday after Sunday, but it's never saturated the parched ground of your soul. To all outward appearances, you are at peace with yourself and others; inwardly, you suffer the private pain of unrelieved guilt. You need more than explanations about the reasons for guilt; you need release.

God's Purpose for True Guilt

The Bible is like a mirror which reflects our true condition. It shows us that God wants to free us from guilt as provided by the remedy in 1 John 1:9: "If we confess our sins, He is faithful and just to forgive us our sins and to cleanse us from all unrighteousness."

God's purpose for guilt is to bring us to a right relationship with Him, to give some moral stability to society, and to guide us in appropriately respecting the rights of other people.[2]

True guilt will alert us when we have done wrong or when we have violated a relationship and need to take corrective measures. That is why a knowledge of God's Word is so essential to living a life in harmony with God and our fellowman. When we know what is pleasing to the Father, then we seek to live according to His guidelines. When the Holy Spirit is given access to our hearts, He controls our impulses and checks our bent to sin.

Walking in the Spirit and living in the light of the Word keeps us sensitive to God's will. This produces what the Bible calls "the fruit of the Spirit"—actions that are loving, kind, peaceful, gentle, long-suffering and patient, self-controlled, and faithful. There is a demonstrated joy that isn't dependent upon circumstances; it is rooted in the strength and stability of God's love.

If guilt is your constant companion, a goad that is merciless and cruel, then you must differentiate between true and false guilt. Review what you have just read because this is the explanation for true guilt. Most of us are drawn to God by the vehicle of true guilt—the recognition that we are sinful, guilty before a righteous God and in need of His mercy and forgiveness. Unless we establish a right relationship with God and experience the grace of God and the freedom we have in Him, we will live under guilt. True guilt will awaken in us the need for forgiveness and change. When we accept God's forgiveness and move on to forgive ourselves and others, then we can let go of guilt and mature.

Satan's Misuse of Guilt

If you still experience guilt, then recognize that anything that God uses, Satan abuses.

In his book *From Guilt to Grace*, Dwight Carlson explains how Satan abuses guilt and beats us over the head with guilty feelings. It is part of his devious strategy to defeat Christians. Satan already has the world in his stranglehold so his scheme is to go after Christians, creating guilt in them. Be aware!

The apostle Peter described Satan as an adversary going about seeking whom he may devour (1 Peter 5:8). He likens him to a hungry, roaring lion, looking for victims to tear apart. In his claws he carries that potential through the use of guilt.

The Bible tells us that Satan is the "accuser of [the] brethren" (Revelation 12:10). That means you are not exempt from his accusations if you are a Christian. When he attacks, you find yourself thinking, "I'm worthless." Or he brings up something from the past that was unpleasant. Or he lays a guilt trip on you because of your children or your mate. Recognize the devil for who he is. He is trying to depress or discourage you. He would blunt your sensibilities. Satan is out to defeat you.

The late A. W. Tozer, a great Bible expositor, wrote a book entitled *I Talk Back to the Devil*. Tozer writes:

The devil makes it his business to keep Christians in bondage, bound and gagged, actually imprisoned in their own grave clothes. He is a dark and sinister foe dedicated to the damnation of humans. . . . Satan has been in this business of intimidating and silencing and oppressing the people of God for a long, long time. . . . [He] is an old dragon who defies us to this hour. . . . I think we had better get free! We must face up to the issues and attitudes and doubts which constitute our fears, that keep us from being happy and victorious Christians with the true liberty of the children of God. We seem to quake about many things.[3]

Why are you feeling guilty? Have you forgotten that Christ took your sin and the penalty of guilt to the cross? Listen to what the apostle Paul says about this:

You were dead in sins, and your sinful desires were not yet cut away. Then he gave you a share in the very life of Christ, for he forgave all your sins, and blotted out the charges proved against you, the list of his commandments which you had not obeyed. He took this list of sins and destroyed it by nailing it to Christ's cross. In this way God took away Satan's power to accuse you of sin, and God openly displayed to the whole world Christ's triumph at the cross where your sins were all taken away (Colossians 2:13-15 TLB).

"Brethren, we have been declared 'Not Guilty!' by the highest court in all the universe," shouted Tozer, and I would echo that statement!

Guilt Trips

It is good to stop and ask yourself what you are feeling guilty about. Try to pinpoint it. Examine it honestly. Ask God for insight (James 1:5). Perhaps He is trying to get your attention about something; you will want to make sure before you dismiss it. Maybe you did slight someone or say something objectionable; perhaps your daughter was right about something she pointed out to you and you resisted and now you feel guilty. If there is justified guilt as a result of some offense or something you've left undone, wisdom demands that you clear it up. That's acting biblically (Matthew 5:23,24).

But if you have given Satan a foothold so that he is magnifying past memories or spiritual failure, then you would be wise to talk back to the devil. Jesus gave us that example (Luke 4:8).

Past failure is no barrier to a relationship with Christ, nor should failure hinder our present, or characterize our future. God knows us better than we know ourselves. He made us! And He doesn't have to wait for information from the accuser! God has a stake in you, and He doesn't want you crippled by guilt. Remember, He declared that "as far as the east is from the west, so far has He removed [your] transgressions from [you]" (Psalm 103:12). The key is to stay in fellowship with Him.

"Brethren, God never meant for us to be kicked around like a football. He wants us to be humble and let Him do the chastening when necessary. But when the devil starts tampering with you, dare to resist him!" wrote Tozer, adding, "I stand for believing in God and defying the devil—and our God loves that kind of courage among His people."[4]

To resolve false guilt, refuse to accept the false belief, refuse to yield to the guilt feelings, and then desensitize yourself to them.[5]

Each of us carries imprints from our childhood into our adult life. These experiences are like tapes that play over and over in our minds; they form a part of our conscience. Actually, conscience is a God-given entity which serves as a regulating agency to bring us to God and to teach us right from wrong. To ignore the conscience is not good; however, if your conscience is continually bringing up things from the past, deal with this slavery.

One Sunday morning after speaking in a church, I was at the altar praying with people. During this time of prayer a gentleman approached me and said, "I'm a medical doctor with a major problem. Seven years ago while I was in medical school, I lived with my homosexual lover. I had been raised in the church, but had long since run away from God.

"Then I attended a conference where you were speaking. On the seventh night, my hardened heart responded to the love of God. Rich, I just couldn't resist the conviction of the Holy Spirit in my life that night. I was delivered and forgiven of my sin. Immediately, I walked away from the immoral relationship that I was involved in. I have been straight for seven years.

"But for seven days a week, 52 weeks a year for seven years the devil has not let me forget what I was. Each day he told me it would just be a matter of time. Each day I felt as though I couldn't change what I was.

"But thank God, this morning God literally did a spiritual surgery in my mind and emotions and delivered me. Rich, these past thoughts that the devil continuously used against me have finally been covered by the blood of Jesus, and I'm free!"

Guilt feelings are the normal response to a violation of our internalized belief system. If those internal beliefs were imprinted negatively, they can impose a dictatorial tyranny on our present response mechanisms. If we are still trying to live up to standards our parents imposed on us as children, we may be in a no-win situation. Then other people may try to impose their will upon us, and though we think for ourselves and judge wisely, when we go against the wishes of someone else, we end up feeling guilty. Many scenarios like this contribute to our immense load of guilt. But if we remember that true guilt is the result of breaking God's absolutes, then we will have a standard whereby we can judge our guilt feelings.

If we haven't learned to deal with the unpleasant emotions of hurt feelings or anger, then we are much more prone to feelings of guilt. Joy-stealing is Satan's business; this is not God's plan for our happiness and fulfillment. We are well-advised to erase the tapes from our childhood that may be causing us private pain and unnecessary guilt. If we deal with our childish thoughts of the past and, if necessary, seek professional Christian counsel, it will help relieve our false guilt.

Parental Guilt

Today many parents of adult children are experiencing a lot of guilt. In responding to Helen Hosier's investigations and questionnaire, one mother wrote:

> Guilt—yes, yes, yes! With every "failure" or unhappiness of my adult children, I've taken upon myself this awful burden of guilt, feeling I've done something to cause it. I tell myself I've failed to give my child the confidence he needs, or the whatever . . . and then remorse sets in and the "If onlys."

Hosier writes:

> It is the cry of a guilt-ridden mother. Almost without exception the parents I've talked to and those responding to the survey indicated in one way or another that they live with guilt. For some it is just a residue of guilt prompted now and then by a painful memory from a "rock bottom" time in their lives. For others it is an enormous problem easily triggered by memories or the demands of children, mates, friends, parents, God, or one's own conscience.[6]

Such guilt is a waste of emotional and mental energy. Sometimes it's anger turned inward. It can even be a form of masochism, i.e., a form of pleasure we derive from being abused or dominated by another person, or from hurting ourselves. It is self-abasement in one way or another.

Such emotional abscesses, pockets of venomous feelings, need to be dealt with. Barbara Johnson, founder of Spatula Ministries (working with parents of homosexuals and others confronted with the problem of homosexuality and private pain), urges those whom she counsels to "drain the pain," and to get rid of these emotional abscesses.[7]

To be rid of the private pain of guilt, pinpoint the reason(s) for guilt, then take steps that will right the wrongs whenever that is possible, alleviate the pain, or do whatever is necessary to restore right relationships.

Parents need to forgive themselves for past failure. God has forgiven them if they've confessed it; now they need to forgive themselves. This will go a long way to defuse parental guilt. They need to work to bring about healing with their adult children if indeed a breach exists.

Guilt with a capital "G" exists and some individuals do have guilt-accepting personalities. The love, forgiveness, and acceptance we have received at the hands of our heavenly Father needs to be extended to ourselves, to our children, and to others. No one needs to be paralyzed by guilt, yet I find Christians who mentally assent to this, but who do not practice it. The consequences of unresolved guilt are too great to ignore.

Guilt and Consequences

The real danger in harboring guilt is that it can destroy one's faith. Satan uses the lust of the body to bind the mind, then so crushes us with guilt that we let go of our faith. That is one of Satan's more subtle tactics. Once the devil fills you with despair, it is easy to overwhelm you with guilt and thus flood your mind with unbelief.

But consider the possibility that if you are experiencing guilt, you may be grieving over that which produced the guilty feelings. The sin-hardened man or woman has no such remorse. If you are grieving this way, clear the matter up. Take care of it. It is God's nature to forgive. He may be calling out to you through your conscience, so listen. If this guilt-trip is one of Satan's tactics, then consider that God is asking you to lay down your guilt. Stop justifying your weaknesses, cease self-condemnation, accept His forgiveness, and move on, guilt-free, with God in control. Are you a prodigal wanting to come home? The Father is waiting! Are you like the woman with a long-standing problem who touched Christ's garment? Reach out. Jesus is there!

Ponder this truth: King David, Peter, and the apostle Paul are three good examples of men who could have been strangled by guilt and lived vastly different lives. David ordered a man killed so he could have the man's wife. Peter denied Jesus in Jesus' most crucial hour. Paul persecuted Christians. But each man accepted responsibility for his sins through the pain of repentance. That led to the peace of forgiveness from the Great Forgiver. Self-acceptance followed as a sweet gift of God because of divine acceptance. Guilt was gone. This kind of private pain would never dominate their lives again.

Guilt is one kind of private pain that is universal. But the Christian must differentiate between true or false guilt and then deal with it. God wants us to rise above the guilt feelings and the pessimism, despair, and other emotions it produces. He wants to display the presence of the supernatural—His own Holy Spirit at work in our lives.

Much guilt relates to the past. The apostle Paul was an example for all: "But one thing I do," he said, "forgetting what is behind and straining toward what is ahead, I press on toward the goal to win the prize for which God has called me heavenward in Christ Jesus" (Philippians 3:13,14 NIV).

We are to learn from the past without being controlled by it. To be "hung up" on our past, nurturing our guilt, will

not accomplish God's purpose in our lives. Paul says it's
sometimes better to forget than to remember.

The thing to remember is who our adversary is. We must
talk back to the devil, then walk on, actuating our faith,
responding to who Christ is. The way to conquer guilt and
fear is to live in blessed day-by-day victory with a conscious
awareness of God's grace. We must look beyond ourselves to
Him who is the source of all strength and power, and then
reach out and extend ourselves to others. We must enlarge
our borders; trust God to conquer the unconquerable for
us.

> Oh that Thou wouldst bless me indeed, and
> enlarge my border, and that Thy hand might be
> with me, and that Thou wouldst keep me from
> harm, that it may not pain me! (1 Chronicles 4:10
> NAS).

Chapter 7

THE DRAGON FACTOR:

Satan and His Bag of Tricks

I'd like to make peace with all the dragons in
my head. . . .
        —Marilee Zdenek and Marge Champion[1]

We've all seen pictures or watched films of dragons—
those mythical monsters, usually represented as large rep-
tiles with wings and claws, breathing out fire and smoke.
They are depicted as towering in rage, incredible in power.

When describing Satan, the Bible refers to him as being
"the dragon, that serpent of old" (Revelation 20:2). Descriptive terminology is used throughout the Old and the
New Testaments. In referring to that future time when God
will execute judgment on both His enemies and His people,
the prophet Isaiah wrote: "In that day the Lord will take his
terrible, swift sword and punish leviathan, the swiftly moving serpent, the coiling, writhing serpent, the dragon of the
sea" (Isaiah 27:1 TLB).

One thing is certain: the dragon is too big for mere man
to tackle. Dragon-fighting calls for someone bigger and
more powerful than the dragon. That someone is God.

The Heat and the Fury of the Dragon

Let's look at the dragons which are mounting ferocious
attacks against God's people today. Let me explain that
Satan is *the* dragon, but there are dragon forces bent on

destroying us. Satan has his helpers and his means of attacking God's people. You can add to the list, but the following are some of those powerful forces which are seeking to destroy us:

- Suppressed anger
- Depression
- Depraved emotions which show themselves in such things as:
  child abuse
  rape
  wife abuse
  incest
  homosexuality
  violent acts of crime
  cruelty
  verbal abuse
- Intimidation by one's superiors, co-workers, or even family members and friends
- Put-downs; psych-out "games"; and similar negatives
- Poor self-image
- Discrimination and second-class treatment
- Deceit and sham; subterfuge and lies; dishonesty
- Immorality
- Fear
- Discouragement
- Health problems
- A deformed value system which can include:
  Busyness
  Materialism
  Conceit; arrogance; an inflated ego
  Conformism to the world
  Wrong views of God, the church, and truth

The list could get very long, but any of these things can cause a lot of private pain, especially if you are being victimized. The trauma and mental anguish of those who have experienced rape, child or wife abuse, or even verbal abuse at the hands of a victimizer is private pain that can hardly be described or understood by those of us who have not been victims.

To be married, for instance, to a man who is a perpetual womanizer, while posing as a model of propriety, would be pain that could lead to despair, devastated confidence, and monumental problems.

After a Sunday morning crusade not too long ago, a woman approached me, saying, "Mr. Wilkerson, what do you do when the head deacon of your church is bringing drugs across the border and selling them at a large profit? What do you do when that deacon is seeing women in the community and no one knows about it? And what do you do, Mr. Wilkerson, when that head deacon is your husband?" After I had a word of prayer with her, she turned and walked sadly away. And I thought to myself, *There is a woman suffering from private pain.*

That woman's problem and resultant pain is not unusual. It's happening, even among our religious leaders. And one of the emotions it produces is the crippling loss of self-worth. Moreover, the sadness it has brought into that home is indescribable. What does a woman do in a situation like that when there are children to support and when she's feeling inadequate, unqualified, incapable of going out to make a living for them? What kind of a future do she and her children have? What does she do with the anger it produces?

Anger is a destructive force that can have devastating effects upon those who harbor it. The Bible tells us not to let the sun go down upon our wrath because stored anger builds pressure. Keeping the lid on our angry feelings requires a great deal of mental and emotional energy— energy that could be used in constructive living. Anger commonly follows a crisis experience. The different reasons for anger pose a threat to emotional well-being which leads to further hurt and more pain.

Depression is a negative emotion that is enervating, depleting our ability to get on with living. Oftentimes depression is the result of seeing ourselves as failures—failures in our work, our parenting, our relationship with our mate, just failure at being a person of worth. Many times such depression is brought on by the experience of rejection when your mate leaves you for "the other person." Depression usually results in a loss of dignity and hope. Many complicating issues further decrease our self-esteem.

Such debilitating forces weaken and devitalize us if we allow them to go unchecked. If we internalize and accept these dragons, we will find ourselves deprived of spiritual vitality.

In reading Betty Esses DeBlase's book *Survivor of a Tarnished Ministry*, I was impressed with the wisdom she showed when she finally had the courage to tackle the dragon that pinned her down. A victim of her husband's multiple infidelities and verbal and physical abuse, Betty's anger finally drove her to seek professional help. Here's what she said:

> There comes a time in many people's lives when they need to recognize that they need help to find solutions to problems that have been eroding their stability. If you are in a relationship that is slowly but surely destroying you, and you are unable to rise above the mire, then you need to reach out for some professional help.

> You must be very selective about the professional help you seek. A strong recommendation from someone you know and respect is your first step toward getting constructive help. I know many people say that if you just trust God, you will never need professional help. Well, I trusted God to see that I found a professional counselor who could help me with my emotional needs just as I would pray for God's help in finding the right doctor for my physical needs.[2]

The Wise Counselor

Betty's wise Christian counselor helped her sort out her life and helped her get back on the road to peace and dignity. He helped her work through her guilt and helped her understand her earlier actions that held her captive to the dragon for 28 sorrowful years. She was able to say, "I thank God that I was finally free from bondage. . . ."

Betty learned that she didn't have to fight the dragon alone; that there were wise Christian counselors who loved her, and that those counselors could be depended upon to help her. If that is your situation, then I urge you to seek professional help.

At times we experience painful letdowns because those we respect and those we put on pedestals fall and fail. Some of our "religious" leaders compromise the truth, fall to the lure of the dragon of materialism, have an inflated view of themselves and an ego problem, and develop an Oedipus complex. In his book *Defeating the Dragons of the World*, Stephen D. Eyre says: "The Christian who lives by the Dragons will experience an inner hollowness and know little of true spiritual reality."[3]

Although I urge Christians to show compassion and love toward the fallen, I would be remiss if I didn't sound the warning for all of us to be aware of the dragons in our midst. "The church that is invaded by the Dragons loses its ability to call a bent world to repentance. There is no witness to God's redemptive kingdom," Eyre says. I couldn't agree more.

Awhile back a minister friend of mine came under attack for alleged sexual affairs. He had a large church and a growing television audience. When I heard these rumors, I totally discounted them. Several months after he seemingly weathered the storm, I preached a series of meetings in his church. For two hours during lunch one day, he and his wife wept saying, "Rich, these rumors are not true. They are lies from Satan himself. My reputation has been tarnished, and my wife and I want to go on record as saying that my personal life and ministry are impeccable. I'd be happy to have my innermost thoughts published to the world."

My co-worker and I promised that we would do everything in our power to dispel these lies wherever our travels took us. Several months later, I heard that this man had resigned his church, admitting to multiple sexual affairs through the years. Immediately I thought back to the many times I had defended him. Now I felt betrayed and incredibly disappointed. Whether it's a fallen television or radio ministry, or a local church, the shame brought upon Christianity is grievous. We should demand and expect honesty, integrity, scruples, ethics, and morality from our spiritual leaders.

What I have just said applies equally to Christian husbands who are supposed to be the spiritual heads of their households, but who often put their wives down and keep them subservient. I meet Christian women whose heartache and private pain is all too common a problem. One young mother of three beautiful children is married to a tyrant but is determined, with God's help, to keep their home together. "I have a life preserver that I put on every day," she said. "It is 2 Corinthians 4:16-18. I refuse to give up."

What do those verses say? Paul, who refused to give up even though he lived in constant danger, wrote, "Though our bodies are dying, our inner strength in the Lord is growing every day. These troubles and sufferings of ours are, after all, quite small and won't last very long. Yet this short time of distress will result in God's richest blessing upon us forever and ever! So we do not look at what we can see right now, the troubles all around us, but we look forward to the joys in heaven which we have not yet seen. The troubles will soon be over, but the joys to come will last forever" (TLB).

Our "religious" leaders, as well as prominent figures in government, are showing quite transparently that the dragon is swishing his tail, snaring victims. It is time for Christian accountability.

Pain: the Raw Material for Wisdom and Joy

James, writing to the Jewish Christians who had scattered to save their very lives, urged them to understand what was happening. In effect, he was saying that suffering and pain are the raw materials God uses to give us His wisdom and joy. Here's what he had to say:

> Dear brothers, is your life full of difficulties and temptations? Then be happy, for when the way is rough, your patience has a chance to grow. So let it grow, and don't try to squirm out of your problems. For when your patience is finally in full bloom, then you will be ready for anything, strong in character, full and complete. If you want to know what God wants you to do, ask him, and he will gladly tell you, for he is always ready to give a bountiful supply of wisdom to all who ask him; he will not resent it (James 1:2-5 TLB).

The woman with the issue of blood found Christ to be a pain-remover. But God is also a pain-sharer. He doesn't always remove our pain, but He provides grace to learn and grow through it. Private pain is one of the ways whereby He imparts wisdom and a strange joy. Pain can be instructive and valuable. The pain of self-revelation comes with a price, but it can lead to an inner peace and joy. It is the joy that comes from trusting the One who is bigger than the dragon.

Ponder this truth: Let the pain you are experiencing be to you as an untapped reservoir, a well of strength. God's method of imparting wisdom and joy is unconventional according to the world's standards, but if you will tap into it, you will find it to be an inexhaustible source of comfort and help.

Knowing that you are in the will of God produces a joy and peace that can't be touched by any of the vicissitudes of life. With God's help, you will feel good about yourself once you have conquered the dragon that has caused you so much pain. Self-surrender is the first step and that is painful. It means, among other things, that you must give up what has come to be your "security blanket."

Remember, the very thing that brought the most pain to the Father-heart of God—the death of His Son—has brought the most hope and joy to believers through all the ages. God had to surrender His Son to insults, blasphemies, cruelties, and finally to crucifixion. Jesus had to surrender Himself to all that. The Father and the Son did that for you. When you go through that kind of pain, then you know how to walk alongside others who are experiencing pain. That's what God is offering to do for you. He is saying to each of you in your private pain, "I will see you through it. I know how to fight dragons."

The story is told of Fanny Crosby who was blinded as a small baby when a doctor administered the wrong medication. Her mother grieved to think of the dark world her little girl would know. But as Fanny grew it was plain to those who knew her that she had an inner joy that completely compensated for her blindness. It was the joy of Christ in her life. The dragon of blindness had no power over her. At eight years of age she wrote:

> O what a happy soul am I!
>   Although I cannot see,
> I am resolved that in this world
>   Contented I will be,
> How many blessings I enjoy
>   That other people don't!
> To weep and sigh because I'm blind,
>   I cannot, and I won't.

Often she would say, "Don't waste sympathy on me—I'm the happiest person alive!" She married a blind Methodist clergyman. They had a child who died as an infant. All her sorrow and victory were poured into her hymns. Whenever she wrote, she would kneel in prayer first and then the words would come spontaneously. During her lifetime she wrote thousands of hymns which are still being sung all over the world. Bravely she accepted her blindness. On her gravestone is engraved: AUNT FANNY . . . SHE HATH DONE WHAT SHE COULD.

Sometimes it seems almost impossible to cooperate with God and to believe that any good can come out of our raw pain. But God's wisdom comes in spite of us. He never abandons His children. Give God time. He is never an idle spectator when His children are in pain.

Section II

THE PROMISE
BEYOND THE PAIN

*AND GOD WILL WIPE AWAY EVERY TEAR
FROM THEIR EYES;
THERE SHALL BE NO MORE DEATH,
NOR SORROW,
NOR CRYING;
AND THERE SHALL BE NO MORE PAIN. . . .*

REVELATION 21:4

Chapter 8

PAINDROPS KEEP FALLING

> Many men owe the grandeur of their lives to
> their tremendous difficulties.
>
> —C. H. Spurgeon

Is pain an enemy to be vanquished or a necessary friend?
When you are in the midst of a fiery experience, you are not
inclined to respond well to that kind of a question. You
might be more inclined to counter with another question:
What redeeming value can there possibly be in this pain?

Much pain seems to be unjust—a young father-to-be
learns that his wife, eight months pregnant, has been killed
by a drunken driver. The driver walks away unhurt. Such
pain often causes people to question the goodness and the
power of God.

A young medical student—one year from graduation
and committed to going to the mission field with his wife—
is drowned on a rafting trip with his father. "Why, God,
why?" I've heard it explained that bereavement is like an
amputation; it never seems to heal. Ask the medical student's parents or his wife and they will tell you this is true.

Think of Job in his bereavement. After the loss of all his
children, instead of cursing God, he blessed God and said,
"The Lord gave, and the Lord has taken away; blessed be
the name of the Lord" (Job 1:21). Job was sitting on an ash
heap. He'd torn his robe and shaved his head, but still he
maintained his integrity and uttered that statement. In the

Bible, except for Christ, there's a strong likelihood that no man suffered more than Job.

But even Job had his moments. He was very human, yet there is no record in the Bible that God condemned him for this. Job hurt deeply and gave expression to his feelings. Moreover, he asked a lot of questions. There are over three hundred questions in the book of Job, many of them asked by Job himself. That's not an unusual reaction to pain. However, when Job and God talked, Job confessed his unworthiness to God and said, "I put my hand over my mouth. . . . I will say no more" (Job 40:4,5 NIV). In other words, Job came to the realization that God has His reasons.

I've heard people say, "When I meet God, the first thing I'm going to ask Him is . . ." Then they will blurt out their question and the pain they are feeling. I believe, however, that when we stand in the presence of our Savior, the questions we have on this side of heaven won't seem important. The Bible assures us that God will wipe away all tears and there will be no more death, nor sorrow, nor crying, and no more pain or suffering in that blessed abode of the righteous who have gone to be with Him (Revelation 21:4).

Someone has described the questions and the responses to life's seeming inequities as "wild words of doubt." The wild words—the rantings and the ravings—should not surprise us. People in crisis need to ventilate, to get it out, to let the pain explode. To suppress one's questions or to silence one's panic, fear, and anger is far more injurious to one's faith than to give honest expression to one's feelings. It is not unusual when someone needs God the most to doubt that God is there or even that He is trustworthy. Pain is the companion of doubt in crisis. But do not be mistaken, as Juanita Ryan points out in her book *Standing By*: "Doubt is not the opposite of faith. Disbelief is the opposite of faith. Doubt is a struggle with faith. To doubt is to be suspended between belief and disbelief."[1]

Doubt can lead to disbelief, but it can also lead to a stronger, deeper faith. We have the testimonies of the saints, in ancient and contemporary history, who have allowed the testing of their faith to produce stronger faith.

George Mueller, a great saint of God, was once asked the best way to have strong faith. This patriarch of faith replied, "The only way to learn strong faith, is to endure great trials. I have learned my faith by standing firm amid severe testings."

Testing times come to each of us. There is no way we can escape trials and the resultant pain. It happens. If it hasn't happened to you already, it will. Such is life. But if we stifle our questions and attempt to suppress our pain with a brave false front, much private inner pain results. That's what I want to look at in this chapter. Paindrops do keep falling. They will rain on you and your loved ones. The time to prepare for life's eventualities is today. John Powell says it so well: "Our yesterdays lie heavily upon our todays, and our todays lie heavily upon our tomorrows."[2]

Charades with God Is Wasted Time

I can't claim originality with that subheading, but it's great. John Powell explains his statement like this:

> There is something so healing about "letting it all hang out" with God. . . . This comfort in the human condition depends for me on whether God will accept me this way or not. . . . So I have to put myself on the line the way I am. Charades with God is wasted time. I have to put myself in the posture of trusting his greatness and understanding. This is the essential beginning of prayer.[3]

In the dialogue of prayer we have an opportunity to let it "all hang out." That may sound irreverent, but God is waiting for us to confess to Him our true and naked selves. Martin Luther's first law in reaching out to God through prayer was: *Don't lie to God!* To say to God, "I don't much like what is happening in my life . . ." is to free ourselves from the lies of prefabricated clichés which are so much a part of many Christians' lives. These lies produce much discomfort and inner private pain. When we know we haven't been totally honest with God, we feel rotten inside. What are we trying to hide anyway? He's God! He knows what we are thinking and feeling. Pretense doesn't free us from private pain. It adds to it.

The game of charades is fun to play with friends at a social gathering; but charades with God is self-defeating and a horrendous waste of time. To pretend that you are handling your private pain well, when inside you are pro- testing, screaming "unfair" or whatever, and that you don't understand, is setting yourself up for a Humpty-Dumpty kind of fall.

A Very Available Help in Time of Trouble

The Bible tells us that "God is our refuge and strength, a very present help in trouble" (Psalm 46:1). That's as consis- tent a theme as any that you will find threaded throughout the Word of God. Among other things, it means that God is a tested help in times of trouble. He is ever-present to help us in our private pain. The kind of help He offers has been well-proven.

Samuel Rutherford said, "Why should I tremble at the plough of my Lord, that maketh deep furrows in my soul? I know He is no idle husbandman; He purposeth a crop."

This pain at the very core of your life is so excruciatingly real. You cannot help but utter the "Why" questions and the "If only . . ." statements. There's nothing wrong with that. Did you know that while Jesus hung on the cross He asked, "Why?": "My God, My God, why have You forsaken Me?" (Matthew 27:46).

I'll never forget the phone call telling me about a 35-year- old man who had come to faith in Christ in our crusade several years back. The man had had a very sordid past, but he was changed by the power of Jesus Christ and became a member of a local evangelical church.

He began studying the Word of God and in time was given a Sunday school class to teach. During this blessed change in his life, he met a beautiful woman in her early thirties who had never been married. She had been raised in the church and had never turned her back on God. Through the course of time, they began dating, then married. Their life together was fantastic. After two years of marriage, a very successful job, and a wonderful volunteer ministry in the church, the man began feeling ill.

He went to the doctor only to discover that he was infected with the AIDS virus, an infection dating back to his days of sin before coming to Christ. His precious wife also discovered that she had AIDS.

As they sat in their pastor's office, all they could say was, "Why? Why? Why?" The man added, "I can understand my having this plague, but what did my wife ever do to deserve this? Why, God? Why?"

God understands all about the whys. But He doesn't want you stuck in the rut of questioning. There must come a time in our praying and crying out to God when we are silent before Him so that He can speak to us. God has some things to say to us when we are hurting. But His gentle touch and His quiet words won't be felt or heard if we continue fighting, questioning, and struggling, without stopping to listen.

God Still Speaks

One of the ways God communicates to us is through His written Word. We will fail to receive the comfort, help, and hope we need if we are neglecting His Word. Perhaps at no time do we need it more than when we are overwhelmed with private pain. To know the God of the Word, through reading His Word, provides strength and stability in our painful circumstances. We are able to draw from that reservoir. Now is the time to start drawing.

When you know that the God of Abraham, Isaac and Jacob, Isaiah and Jeremiah, David, Peter, James and John, and the apostle Paul actually spoke to them, that He pursued them, that He strengthened their faith and took them through their trials, *then you know* that you have a God who is trustworthy, big enough to come to your rescue.

He can touch and calm your turbulent emotions. He can put new strength into your will. He can calm the sea and quiet the waves that threaten to slosh into your "boat" and drown you. He doesn't close doors without providing new opportunities to trust Him. He's felt your tug; it's reached His heart, not just His garment. Now He wants to communicate to you. Listen to Him for His words to you can be life-changing. (See Appendix in the back of this book).

Pain: an Enemy or a Friend?

One of the ways God speaks to us is through life's circumstances. It is, as C. S. Lewis said, His megaphone to get our attention. God would have us know that suffering is not a topic for speculation. It is an opportunity to learn compassion, to become victors instead of victims. We can either master suffering or be servants to it. Our private pain can be a friend.

The apostle Paul understood this. He wrote to the Christians at Corinth and explained: "Praise be to the God and Father of our Lord Jesus Christ, the Father of compassion and the God of all comfort, who comforts us in all our troubles, so that we can comfort those in any trouble with the comfort we ourselves have received from God" (2 Corinthians 1:3,4 NIV).

Rabbi Harold Kushner caused people to think with his book *When Bad Things Happen to Good People*. The "why" of that question has been the subject of an ongoing debate for centuries. I believe Kushner's reason for writing it was to help people who hurt and are perplexed by life's problems and inequities. But a pastor came along and wrote a book with a similar title that puts the question in better perspective. Warren Wiersbe's book *Why Us? When Bad Things Happen to God's People* offers faith-bolstering insight to help us handle suffering in realistic and effective ways. Wiersbe's approach is to show that God uses our present suffering as a channel for ultimate blessing. And therein lies the answer to the question posed at the outset of this chapter: *Is pain an enemy to be vanquished or a necessary friend?*

Can you believe that God is providentially at work in this world and in your life, and that the events that come into your experience are appointments, not accidents—that these things are the outworking of His plan for you?

Sometimes things happen that are not in accordance with His perfect will for our lives. But we live in an imperfect world where sin abounds. We cannot always escape the crushing impact of that, nor do we always have control of the circumstances surrounding us. A car careens around the corner and smashes into a friend's car. Your young friend is permanently disabled. Things of this nature happen and Christians are not exempt from experiencing pain that accompanies tragedy.

"Couldn't God have prevented it?" someone asks. Yes, but we live in a fallen world where tragedies and heartbreaks exist. The promise is that "all things work together for good to those who love God, to those who are the called according to His purpose" (Romans 8:28).

Perhaps you've heard it emphasized that this verse doesn't say that all things are good. That's important. But what God does promise is that if we allow Him, He will take these painful things and work them together for our ultimate good. He hasn't vanquished the pain or the effects that pain has brought into your life, or the lives of loved ones; but given access to our lives, God will bind up the wounds that the pain has inflicted, and, in time, good can come out of it. Pain can be our teacher.

> Good pain is pain that teaches us, that pushes
> our roots deep enough so that we do not have to

depend wholly upon the watering of others. Next to love and encouragement, pain is a necessity of growth. Suffering can strip away the frivolous, the excess, the transitory from our lives. We learn, for example, that money or things are a poor substitute for love. In our distress, we discover that transitory possessions do not feed our spirits any more than junk food nourishes our bodies.[4]

Lutheran theologian Robert M. Herhold cautions that when we look upon pain as an archenemy to escape from or to defeat at all costs, then we are not prepared to learn from it. When all our energy goes into avoiding or fighting suffering, then the battle becomes a source of despair as we discover it is impossible to eliminate all pain.

We have seen people attempt to escape private pain with their addictive habits (discussed in chapter 5). We've also seen how failing to do battle with the dragon can immobilize us and lead us into despair, depression, anger, discouragement, or many other debilitating emotions (see chapter 7).

In these and other ways, pain becomes our enemy. We won't miss the message that pain would have us learn if we stop running from it, fighting it, or seeking to remove it, and simply listen to it. Because we live in a world of instant gratification and satisfaction, we have the false notion that there should be instant relief from pain. To escape before we learn from the hurt is to deprive ourselves of valuable lessons at the hand of our Friend.

But we want answers and when we can't make sense out of our pain we rail at God. God—not the problem, not the pain—becomes our enemy. We run the risk of missing out on God's friendship, the strength of His comfort and presence, and the blessing that can come in the acceptance of that pain. Instead, in blaming God, we are left with bitterness, despair, and private pain.

Cruel or Compassionate

The kindest, most sympathetic, helpful, and understand-ing people I have met have been those individuals who have suffered the most. Often someone will take me aside and say, "Let me tell you something about that man [or woman] you just talked to."

I am grateful I can tell you that many people with private pain have come to terms with their pain. These are the compassionate ones. Compassionate people come in all shapes, colors, sizes, and, amazingly, in all ages.

I had just finished a junior high school assembly and was leaving the auditorium when the principal approached my friend and said, "Wilkerson's words today brought back the memory of a former student."

He then told my friend, "Last year I had an eighth grade, 13-year-old student, who started showing up at school every day *an hour late*. I couldn't get this boy to come to school on time.

"First, I sent notes home to his parents. He would bring the note back the next day *signed* by his parents . . . *an hour late!* Secondly, I paddled the young man. The next day he showed up to school . . . *an hour late*. Thirdly, I kept the boy after school for days. No matter, every day he was still *an hour late*. Finally, after two months of being tardy to school everyday, I suspended the young man from school for three days. On the fourth day he returned to school from suspen-sion and he was *ONE HOUR LATE!*

"I just couldn't take it anymore, so the next day I went to the welfare department. Welfare agents accompanied me to the boy's home. We walked up to the front door and knocked. No one answered, so I turned the doorknob. It was open so we walked in and what we found wasn't very pretty.

"Two months earlier, while he was at school, the boy's parents left home. They left two months' worth of groceries in the cupboards and refrigerator, but they left.

"The boy had no idea where his parents were. He was too ashamed to tell me about his problem. He was tardy to school each day because at the crack of dawn he would get his eight-year-old sister and six-year-old brother out of bed.

"He would get them bathed and dressed for school. He would cook them their morning breakfast and clean up the mess. Then this big, loving 13-year-old brother would take his eight-year-old sister in one hand and his six-year-old brother in the other hand, and walk them to their elementary school so they would get there on time, safely, and not get in trouble.

"Once there, he would kiss them good-bye and turn and run the two miles to our junior high school. But, by the time he arrived, he would be *ONE HOUR LATE*."

The principal concluded, "I felt so bad because I had paddled that boy, I had suspended that boy, and I had been rude to that boy all for doing what his big mom and dad didn't have enough love to do. The boy loved his little brother and sister enough that he was willing to 'stay, when the staying gets tough'."

In the middle of his "private pain" that 13-year-old boy had learned compassion.

There are exceptions, of course. Sometimes a chain reaction can set in whereby someone suffering pain goes on to inflict pain on others. This is the problem with many child abusers—they themselves are the victims of abuse at the hands of someone. Sometimes parents are guilty of this. Because they refused to listen to the messenger of pain, treating it as an enemy, they did not let it make them wise. Neglected pain can make us cruel and the cycle of pain can be passed down from one generation to another. Many parents were once brutalized children.

The hope is that our pain will soak in. All of our instincts rebel against feeling the hurt we felt as children. We struggle to forget or repress our pain. . . . There is no inexorable law saying that because we were hurt, we must hurt in return. The gospel means that suffering can produce sensitivity, patience, and kindness, not necessarily more suffering. We break through to the other side of the pain and experience the awful grace of God when we see ourselves in others and recognize the pain on their faces as our own.[5]

If you have been bruised and battered, be restored by the healing grace that God offers. Life is far too short to go around making others suffer for our own hurt. We have it within our power to make the paindrops stop falling—drops that are so injurious to others and ourselves—when we allow God's healing grace to seep into our hearts. I pray that this will be your experience.

Paindrops of Blessing

"God has made me fruitful in the land of my suffering" (Genesis 41:52 NIV). Without looking, can you guess who said that?

It was Joseph who had more painful experiences than all the other sons of Jacob. How do you think he felt when his brothers stripped him of the coat of many colors which his father had given him? What did he think when they dropped him in an empty cistern? And how do you think he felt when they changed their minds, pulled him out, and sold him to the Ishmaelites? Later, you will recall, he was sold into slavery in Egypt. Try and imagine the turmoil this young man went through—the pain of being rejected by his own brothers; the long years of separation from his beloved father, Jacob; the uncertainty, the loneliness, the fear. But do you know what the Holy Spirit said of Joseph when he spoke through his father? Before his death as Jacob blessed his sons, he said of Joseph, "Joseph is a fruitful vine . . . near a spring, whose branches climb over a wall" (Genesis 49:22 NIV).

Joseph acknowledged that God had made him fruitful. What a beautiful analogy. The Bible gives us several metaphors for suffering and pain. One of these is the agricultural image and that of the vineyard. In John 15:5 Jesus compared His relationship with His followers as that of the vine to the branches. By abiding in Him, the vine, Jesus said we would bear much fruit: "This is to my Father's glory, that you bear much fruit, showing yourselves to be my disciples" (John 15:8 NIV). Branches don't bear fruit unless they are pruned; it is the pruned vine that produces the most lush grapes. "My Father is the gardener," Jesus said. "He cuts off every branch in me that bears no fruit, while every branch that does bear fruit he trims clean so that it will be even more fruitful" (John 15:1,2 NIV).

Pruning is painful to us, but pruning is an essential process in the Father's hands if our lives are to yield rich harvests—fruit that lasts.

The agricultural metaphor also suggests plowing. It is the plowed field that brings forth crops. An unknown poet wrote:

> The dark brown mould's upturned
> By the sharp-pointed plow;
> And I've a lesson learned.
>
> My life is but a field,
> Stretched out beneath God's sky,
> Some harvest rich to yield.
>
> Where grows the golden grain?
> Where faith? Where sympathy?
> In a furrow cut by pain.

And what would this earth be like without showers to water the planted crops, the vegetation and flowers? What a barren world it would be without rain. Remember Longfellow's words: "Into each life some rain must fall."

There's another bit of verse that says, "It isn't raining rain for me, it's raining daffodils. . . ."

Is it raining rain for you, or is it raining blessing? An unknown writer said:

> Testings are raining upon me which seem beyond my power to endure. Disappointments are raining fast, to the utter defeat of all my chosen plans. Bereavements are raining into my life which are making my shrinking heart quiver in its intensity of suffering. The rain of affliction is surely beating down upon my soul these days.

To which another writer replied:

> Friend, you are mistaken. It isn't raining rain for you. It's raining blessing. For, if you will but believe your Father's Word, under that beating rain are springing up spiritual flowers of such fragrance and beauty as never before grew in that stormless, unchastened life of yours.
>
> You indeed see the rain. But do you see also the flowers? You are pained by the testings. But God sees the sweet flower of faith which is upspringing in your life under those very trials.
>
> You shrink from the suffering. But God sees the tender compassion for other sufferers which is finding birth in your soul.
>
> Your heart winces under the sore bereavement. But God sees the deepening and enriching which that sorrow has brought to you.
>
> It isn't raining afflictions for you. It is raining tenderness, love, compassion, patience, and a thousand other flowers and fruits of the blessed Spirit, which are bringing into your life such a spiritual enrichment as all the fullness of worldly

prosperity and ease was never able to beget in your innermost soul.[6]

Mrs. Cowman, who compiled the devotional book *Streams In The Desert* had inscribed on the frontpiece of this devotional, "Through waves, and clouds, and storms, He gently clears the way."

Storms can be destructive and often strike without much warning. Whether those storms are in nature, or whether they are storms that sweep into our personal lives with a terrible ferocity, in their wake they can leave a lot of pain. The imagery of storms, floods, lightning, hail, snow, clouds, and tempestuous seas is used throughout the Bible.

We don't always escape the storms. But what's important to remember is who controls the storms. After mournful complaining, the disciples learned that with Christ in the vessel they could sail through the storm. We learn from the storms that smashed into David's life that he was a better man after the storms. So was Job. It took a storm at sea and a prayer meeting from the belly of a whale to bring Jonah back to his senses: "All your waves and breakers swept over me" (Jonah 2:3 NIV).

Someone wisely said, "If you wish your neighbors to see what God is like, let them see what He can make you like. The paindrops and the storms that blow into our lives provide just such opportunities." The psalmist could say, "O God, my heart is steadfast" (Psalm 108:1). He could proclaim this with conviction because, in spite of his private pain, he had learned this magnificent truth: "Through God [I can] do valiantly" (v. 13).

Ponder this truth: Learning from our private pain is part of the healing. We do not welcome the "paindrops that keep falling." But if we stop begging to be pain-free, if we give up our struggling, dissenting, and complaining, and if we listen to God and learn what He is trying to teach us, then there is a strong likelihood that we will emerge stronger and more compassionate.

> . . . pain which
> cannot forget, falls drop by drop
> upon the heart until, in our own despair,
> against our will, comes wisdom through
> the awful grace of God.[7]

Where do you go when the storm clouds threaten? David wrote: "O God . . . I am trusting you! I will hide beneath the shadow of your wings until this storm is past. I will cry to the God of heaven who does such wonders for me" (Psalm 57:1,2 TLB).

> Thanks be to Thee, my Lord Jesus Christ,
> For all the benefits which Thou hast given me.
> For all the pains and insults which thou hast
>   borne for me.
> O, most merciful Redeemer, Friend and Brother,
> May I know Thee more clearly,
> Love Thee more dearly,
> And follow Thee more nearly.
> —Richard Bishop of Chichester

Chapter 9

Oh, the Thorns!

It's the thorns that bug us. . . .
　　　　　　　　—Charles R. Swindoll[1]

Almost everyone knows the discomfort that accompanies getting a thorn in your finger. We love the smell and the beauty of roses, but we don't like the thorns. Strange, that something as beautiful and fragrant as a rose should come with thorns. Have you ever thought about that?

There's something paradoxical about that. Roses bloom on thorny stems. It's analogous to life, and the Bible talks about it.

The most familiar reference to thorns is the apostle Paul's "thorn in the flesh" (2 Corinthians 12:7). But the eleventh chapter of 2 Corinthians precedes the twelfth. Paul's letters allude to his afflictions and adversities. Talk about private pain. Here was a man who had come to Damascus with all the pomp and pride of a distinguished representative of the Jewish supreme council. On the way, he was stricken by a blinding light which led to his encounter with Christ and his remarkable conversion experience. Later, Paul was compelled to slink away in the darkness like a hunted thief, let down over the city wall in a basket. It was only one in a series of narrow escapes he was to endure. But it was embarrassing. It was private pain. *Surely, God, You could have treated me better*. Was that what he was thinking? Hardly. Not this man who endured so much suffering and pain. Yet, in his long recital of problems in 2 Corinthians 11, he closes by referring to his Damascus-basket experience. Undoubtedly, it left quite an impression on the apostle. Private pain will leave its mark.

Enforced Boasting

Boasting is folly. There are few occasions when a person is justified in boasting. To give a proud rehearsal of one's attainments or to show off one's possessions smacks of poor taste, selfishness, and utter pretentiousness. The false apostles of Paul's day, masquerading as apostles of Christ, were seeking to discredit Paul and to lead the Corinthian church astray. Slander was one of their weapons. The fruit of Paul's labor was being destroyed by these false teachers. The self-glorification of those who were wreaking havoc in the church needed answers. Paul said to the Corinthians, "I am jealous over you with godly jealousy" (2 Corinthians 11:2 KJV).

Necessity, rather than expediency, compelled the apostle to boast. Unlike his enemies, he bragged only in his weakness, stating that through his weakness the power of Christ was manifested. In order to shame his enemies, and the enemies of the cross, Paul found it necessary to recite the labors, sufferings, and spiritual privileges that were his by apostleship.

The Extent of Paul's Pain

> Let no one take me for a fool. But if you do, then receive me just as you would a fool, so that I may do a little boasting. . . . I have worked much harder [than the false teachers], been in prison more frequently, been flogged more severely, and been exposed to death again and again (2 Corinthians 11:16,23 NIV).

Beatings: Beatings were a commonplace experience for Paul who endured "stripes above measure." "Five times I received from the Jews the forty lashes minus one. Three times I was beaten with rods" (vv. 24, 25 NIV). Forty was the maximum number of stripes allowed by Jewish law; the practice was to stop at 39 to avoid a violation. The Roman method was to beat with rods.

Stonings: "Once I was stoned" (v. 25 NIV), he explained.

Shipwrecks: "Three times I was shipwrecked" (v. 25 NIV).

Dangerous Travels: "I have been constantly on the move. I have been in danger from rivers, in danger from bandits, in danger from my own countrymen, in danger from Gentiles; in danger in the city . . . in the country . . . at sea . . . and in danger from false brothers" (v. 26 NIV).

The review of Paul's sufferings includes mention of hunger, sleeplessness, thirst, coldness, and nakedness (v. 27). He speaks of his concern for all the churches (v. 28). He gives us a glimpse of his pastoral heart when he shares the pain of those who are weak and who are easily led into sin (v. 29).

I read all that and I shake my head in amazement. How did you stand all that, Paul, and not crack up? Had God abandoned you? Did you ever doubt God? Did questions cross your mind? Did you ask, *Why me, God? I'm one of yours!*

But I have to be honest. I don't think Paul asked those questions. Paul goes on to explain about the visions and revelations he'd had—incredible experiences that caught him up to "the third heaven" (2 Corinthians 12:2 NIV). He really did have something to boast about, but that's not what he was doing. He related his aversion to boasting, but said that it was necessary. And all this precedes Paul's reference to his "thorn in the flesh."

"Oh, the Thorn!"

To keep me from becoming conceited because of these surpassingly great revelations, there was

given me a thorn in my flesh, a messenger of
Satan, to torment me. Three times I pleaded with
the Lord to take it away from me. But he said to
me, "My grace is sufficient for you, for my power
is made perfect in weakness." Therefore I will
boast all the more gladly about my weaknesses, so
that Christ's power may rest on me. That is why,
for Christ's sake, I delight in weaknesses, in insults, in hardships, in persecutions, in difficulties.
For when I am weak, then I am strong (2 Corinthians 12:7-10 NIV).

Much speculation surrounds Paul's narrative. First, what
is meant by his being caught up into the third heaven? In
part, I think it occurred that Paul might receive divine
revelation from God; this would prepare Paul to face all
that awaited him. An ordinary man might be tempted to
boast about his "experience," but over and over Paul insists
that this is not his intent. Rather, Paul tells the reader that to
keep him from the temptation of boasting and of being
exalted above measure, he was given this "thorn in the
flesh."

Second, what was that thorn? Spiritual weakness? Moral
temptation? Or physical disease so humiliating, agonizing,
and incurable that Paul described it as literally coming as "a
messenger of Satan"? Some translate the word *thorn* as
meaning *stake*—an agony so excruciating as to be depicted
by the barbarous custom of impaling captives or criminals
by driving stakes through their quivering bodies. Paul anguished about this. You are not alone in anguishing about
your private pain. Paul was your predecessor in this whole
business.

Something Better than Thorn Removal

Notice that Paul pleaded with God three times to have
the thorn removed. He wanted relief! He didn't even pray

for the grace to endure it; he just begged for its removal. God was silent.

Have you experienced what appears to be stony silence from God? How do you think Paul felt? God was preparing Paul for His special word to him. Paul needed to quietly wait upon God. That is not easy. We want answers now. Does all this seem familiar to you?

Finally, God's answer came to Paul. In effect God promised to give Paul something better. "My grace is sufficient for you, for My strength is made perfect in weakness" (v. 9).

All-sufficient Grace

Grace was and is a tremendous gift. The verb tense used in God's reply to Paul indicated a sustaining grace. It would be a continuous supply, one Paul could accept for his whole life. That's what is available to any of us who live with private pain. For all the hours of agony and the desperate cries of every suffering soul, these words ring across the centuries as powerfully as they did when the apostle Paul first heard them. God's people have an inexhaustible supply of all they need because of this gift of grace (see Appendix). Grace is undeserved favor! Whatever we receive, we don't deserve, earn, or merit. It comes because of what Christ did on the cross.

Paul took comfort from those words as we must do. We are so slow to learn that we need the thorn(s) to keep us from becoming self-sufficient. Always we are thrust back upon God's reservoir of all-sufficient grace. For God to take away our thorn(s) would be to deprive us of the privilege of claiming His grace. Besides, what Paul received was more than enough to endure the thorn; it made him stronger than he would have been without it. "For when I am weak, then I am strong," Paul said. Dependence upon God brings strength. God gives *us* opportunity to experience His strength in our weaknesses.

The story is told of Dr. Moon, of Brighton, England, who

was stricken with blindness. He said: "Lord, I accept this *talent* of blindness from Thee. Help me to use it for Thy glory that at Thy coming Thou mayest receive Thine own with usury." Then God enabled him to invent the Moon Alphabet for the blind. Because of this, thousands of blind people were enabled to read the Bible; many of them came to know Christ. Would that have happened without Dr. Moon's thorn?

Another blind preacher, George Matheson, wrote the much-loved old hymn "O Love That Wilt Not Let Me Go." Would this great man of God have written that hymn had he not found meaning in his thorn? Read these words:

> O Love that wilt not let me go,
> I rest my weary soul in Thee,
> I give Thee back the life I owe,
> That in thine ocean depths its flow
> May richer, fuller be.
>
> O Light that followest all my way,
> I yield my flickering torch to Thee
> My heart restores its borrowed ray,
> That in Thy sunshine's blaze its day
> May brighter, fairer be.
>
> O Joy that seekest me through pain,
> I cannot close my heart to Thee,
> I trace the rainbow through the rain
> And feel the promise is not vain,
> That morn shall tearless be.
>
> O Cross that liftest up my head,
> I dare not ask to fly from Thee,
> I lay in dust life's glory dead,
> And from the ground there blossoms red,
> Life that shall endless be.

Ponder this truth: At the outset of this chapter I referred to the beauty of roses, but also to their thorns. This devotional was brought to my attention and it conveys a powerful message:

> We must through many tribulations enter the kingdom of God (Acts 14:22).

The best things of life come out of wounding. Wheat is crushed before it becomes bread. Incense must be cast upon the fire before its odors are set free. The ground must be broken with the sharp plough before it is ready to receive the seed. It is the broken heart that pleases God. The sweetest joys in life are the fruits of sorrow. Human nature seems to need suffering to fit it for being a blessing to the world.

> Beside my cottage door it grows,
> The loveliest, daintiest flower that blows,
> A sweetbriar rose.
>
> At dewy morn or twilight's close,
> The rarest perfume from it flows,
> This strange wild rose.
>
> But when the rain-drops on it beat,
> Ah, then, its odors grow more sweet,
> About my feet.
>
> Ofttimes with loving tenderness,
> Its soft green leaves I gently press,
> In sweet caress.
>
> A still more wondrous fragrance flows
> The more my fingers close
> And crush the rose.

Dear Lord, oh, let my life be so
Its perfume when tempests blow,
The sweeter flow.

And should it be Thy blessed will,
With crushing grief my soul to fill,
Press harder still.

And while its dying fragrance flows
I'll whisper low, "He loves and knows
His crushed briar rose."[2]

Would Paul have known the strength he speaks about without the thorn? Paul's acceptance of his thorn was not in a stoic manner. If it had been, it would have been a graceless form of suffering. Paul discovered the secret of bearing crushing private pain with courage and dignity. He recognized that it was the means by which God would reveal His power through him—that he, Paul, had been chosen to bear this particular thorn.

If you wonder about the thorns that come into your life and you want to blame God and lash out at Him, look at God's sufficient grace again. God did not give Paul the thorn, but God did choose to leave it there and to use it for Paul's good. What if Paul had insisted that only the removal of the thorn would satisfy him? How bereft Paul would have been, as well as all of us who have derived comfort and help from God's all-sufficient grace. "Grace and power come to us not despite the suffering, but often because of it."[3]

Katharina Von Schlegel wrote the beautiful words of this song:

Be still, my soul: the Lord is on thy side;
Bear patiently the cross of grief or pain;
Leave to thy God to order and provide;
In every change He faithful will remain.
Be still, my soul; thy best, thy heavenly Friend

Perry Tanksley penned these words which remind us of Christ's thorns:

> A person's greatness can't be hid
> But comes in many forms;
> Sometimes it comes through sunshine days,
> Sometimes it comes through storms
> A person's greatness is revealed
> In many, many ways;
> Sometimes it shines when we are cursed,
> Sometimes it's when we're praised.
> A person's greatness will be seen
> When fame his name adorns;
> Sometimes it comes in other ways;
> For Christ it gleamed through thorns.[4]

Never forget, it was a crown of thorns which was placed upon the head of our dear Savior. Why should we shrink from our thorns? Why not try thanking God for your thorn?

George Matheson wrote:

> My God, I have never thanked Thee for my thorns. I have thanked Thee a thousand times for my *roses*, but not once for my *thorns*. I have looked forward to a world where I shall get compensation for my cross: but I have never thought of my cross as itself a present glory. Teach me the glory of my cross: teach me the value of my thorn. Shew me that I have climbed to Thee by the path of pain. Shew me that my tears have made my rainbow.

Chapter 10

SUFFERING THE TOOL; CHARACTER THE PRODUCT

> The central challenge in our lives is not to explain suffering, but rather to be the kind of people who can face suffering and make it work for us and not against us. . . . In other words, character doesn't come cheaply! The trials of our life can be God's tools for engraving His image on our character.
>
> —Warren W. Wiersbe[1]

I have learned a lot about private pain, about suffering, and about myself in the course of writing this book. I may not have experienced your kind of private pain. And, of course, I am still learning about pain. But I have experienced enough in the shared grief I've borne with others to know that much private pain exists. I hurt for those who hurt. I don't have to bear the same kind of pain or suffer in the same degree in order to have empathy and to be a comforter.

Some of you bear up under your private pain with beautiful courage, composure, and demonstrated faith. Others, while bearing up under it, struggle intensely and their faith wavers. Regardless of where you stand in your experience with private pain, you are not alone. First of all, God is with you in your private pain. Second, others—your brothers and sisters in the Lord—do not want you to anguish alone.

Much private pain is just that—private, unshared, carried

alone. Sometimes it's pride that keeps us from reaching out to others. That can bring desolation and despair, and I believe it can be contradictory to God's Word. I have already referred to the apostle Paul's declaration in 2 Corinthians that we are to comfort those in any trouble with the comfort we ourselves have received from God. We deprive others of being comforters when we are unwilling to share with them what is causing us pain. We need to know that others are praying for us and standing with us. We need the kind of help and comfort God would like to provide for us through them because of what they've already experienced.

Paul said we are to rejoice with those who rejoice, and to mourn with those who mourn (Romans 12:15). The idea is that we are to share with others in both the good and the bad things that come into our lives. This doesn't give us license to inflict needless concern on our friends and family. We are to shun self-pity or calling attention to ourselves for selfish reasons. (We can all think of instances where this has happened and does happen.)

One important lesson God would have us learn from our private pain is that He wants to comfort us and provide the needed inner stability to stand up, whether He removes the pain, or gives us the strength to live with a "thorn." Then, He wants us to stand alongside others and offer them what we have learned from our own experience(s). We are to give unfailing love and acceptance. This is what it means to be a "comforter." When we can do that, then from the raw material of our own suffering, we see that God has developed character within us.

The Master Craftsman: Sculpting and the Sculpted

The title of this chapter comes from something Warren Wiersbe said in his book *Why Us? When Bad Things Happen to God's People*. Wiersbe refers to God as "the Master Craftsman" and says that suffering is one of the tools He uses to refine character. According to Wiersbe, "There is a sense in which suffering helps to make a man or a woman; but there is also a sense in which suffering reveals what they are made of."[2]

We've been looking at some of the ways people deal with their private pain. We've seen the emotional isolation they impose upon themselves or that others impose upon them. We've seen the loneliness that results. We've examined the risk factor—the rejection they fear, the friendlessness they endure, the despair and feelings of hopelessness. We've seen the bondage and secrecy that's become so much a part of their pain; and we've seen the guilt, and the dragons, and besetting sins that stalk people with brutal intensity. Resistance, a defiant attitude toward God, resignation that gives up on God, life, and other people—all these things prevent God from using suffering to build character into our lives. "Man must, with God's help, be the sculptor."[3] Wiersbe refers to a statement by Alexis Carell: "Man is both the marble and the sculptor."

But Helen Hosier says that God is the "great Master Sculptor who lovingly and purposefully chisels, carves, and polishes every one of us to be His precious gems—chipping, carving, and sculpting are all necessary by a craftsman if a gem is to emerge a thing of beauty."[4]

To cooperate with God's intent is to take the private pain and do something with it. That makes sculptors of us. My Grandmother Wilkerson was one of the most compassionate people I've ever known. She always had enough love to go around for everyone—including her eight children and 21 grandchildren.

My Grandfather Wilkerson died in 1963. Grandmother had been living alone for several years when she met a widowed minister named Harvey Krist. By divine appointment, they were eventually married.

God gave them many years of ministry and companionship together. But in the final two years of my grandmother's life, my step-grandfather Krist was the most loving soul imaginable.

Although Grandmother suffered terribly from Alzheimer's disease, Grandfather Krist would not allow her to be placed in a convalescent home. Daily he tended to her every need—the same kind of care that is needed for an infant child. Grandmother eventually became violent and abusive. Of course, she had no idea what she was doing.

Still Grandfather responded with the most loving and gentle care. He would make excuses for her and apologize for her. He would say, "If I was in her condition, she would do it for me." I could see the character of Christ developed in Grandfather's life, and I prayed that God would perfect His character in me as he had in Grandfather Krist's life.

In *My Utmost for His Highest*, Oswald Chambers reminds us that there is no such thing as a private life for a man or woman who is brought into fellowship with Jesus Christ's sufferings:

> God breaks up the private life of His saints, and makes it a thoroughfare for the world on the one hand and for Himself on the other. We are not sanctified [set apart to be made productive of spiritual blessing] for ourselves, we are called into the fellowship of the Gospel, and things happen which have nothing to do with us, God is getting us into fellowship with Himself. Let Him have His way, if you do not, instead of being of the slightest use to God in His redemptive work in the world, you will be a hindrance and a clog.[5]

Chambers asks,

> Why shouldn't we go through heartbreaks? Through these doorways God is opening up ways of fellowship with His Son. Most of us fall and collapse at the first grip of pain; we sit down on the threshhold of God's purpose and die away of

self-pity. . . . But God comes with the grip of the pierced hand of His Son, and says—"Enter into fellowship with Me; arise and shine." If through a broken heart God can bring His purpose to pass in the world, then thank Him for breaking your heart.[6]

You may think that is rather harsh, but I must tell you, on the basis of my study of the Word of God, that this is in keeping with Romans 5:1-5. Paul tells us that suffering produces perseverance; perseverance, character; and character, hope.

In Psalm 18, David looked back at all his private pain— being demeaned by members of his own family, years of persecution, fleeing from the wrath of jealous King Saul, and living in exile. All of this and much more and yet David could say, "Thy providence makes me great" (v. 35 NEB). David could just as well have said, "The pain you allowed to come into my life has made me great." Previous verses in that psalm portray some of what he went through. (Read it; you will be amazed.)

While pastoring in the state of California, I met Willard Spencer, a man who forever influenced my life for God. I always called him Brother Spencer. Brother Spencer was a tall, big-boned woodsman from the state of Oregon, a pioneer pastor in that state for many years. The apostle Paul had a tent-making business to support his personal ministry for Christ; Brother Spencer was a logger. His logging helped him accomplish the work God had called him to.

Spencer would go into a new area, get a job logging, and begin leading people to Jesus. Somehow he'd get enough people together to form a little church. Once the membership was large enough to support a pastor, Brother Spencer would have a young pastor take over the church. Then Spencer and his family would move on to the next place to pioneer another church.

In one little town, Brother Spencer and several other loggers were involved in a chemical explosion. Spencer and his friends were permanently disabled. By the time I met him, Brother Spencer had suffered greatly; he had had one kidney removed and was about to lose the second one.

I visited him once a week at his house. He would quote Scripture and preach me sermons. We'd pray together. Then I'd leave his presence feeling as though I were the sick person who had just been visited.

Eventually, Brother Spencer had his second kidney removed. For nearly two years, he spent every other day on a dialysis machine. Finally, he was taken to the hospital for the last time. During his final days, I visited Brother Spencer for the last time.

I walked into the hospital room and looked at that man who had felled giant redwoods singlehandedly. Now he lay in an emaciated state, barely alive. A grey-green cast covered his face; he couldn't move.

When he heard me approach, a huge smile crossed his face from east to west. He said quietly, "How is my preacher son doing today?" I said, "Just fine, Brother Spencer."

"It won't be long now, Rich, 'til I'll see my Jesus face to face."

For the next 30 minutes, he struggled to instruct me in the ways of the Lord. Then, he reached for my hand. "Come here, son," he said in a whisper, "I want to sing my testimony and prayer to you one last time. It has been my prayer through the years. Promise me, son, that it will be yours as well." I promised.

Then he began to sing the old chorus:

O to be like Thee
O to be like Thee
Blessed redeemer, pure as Thou art
Come in Thy sweetness
Come in Thy fullness

> Stamp Thine own image
> Deep on my heart.

He fell asleep. I stood up with tears streaming down my cheeks. For a brief moment, I thought I saw the picture of Christ where Brother Spencer had been lying. The pain and suffering had produced perfection once again.

God is in the character-building business. Some may not like that implication. But look at Job who was tested like no other biblical character, and he passed the tests. Could you, like Job, affirm, "But he knows the way that I take; when he has tested me, I will come forth as gold" (Job 23:10 NIV). God can be trusted to use the right tools to shape our lives.

Oswald Chambers says, "Whenever God has dumped you down in circumstances, pray. . . ." We have access to the Father to see us through. "If you are going through a time of discouragement, there is a big personal enlargement ahead." Can you, in faith, believe that?

Jude, the New Testament writer believed to be the brother of our Lord, warned the early Christians about false teachers and the persecution they could expect. Jude urged the believers to build themselves up in their faith, to pray without ceasing, and to keep themselves in the love of God (vv. 20, 21). This is the essential posture for that man or woman whose hope is in God; that hope doesn't have to be a distant prospect, but it can be a present reality.

The situation for many of you who read this book may seem hopeless from a strictly human perspective. You've been pushed to the brink. Your back is up against the proverbial wall. You're at the wire. But I offer you the certainty that God is in this experience with you!

I stake my whole being on that certainty. God has not forgotten you. He's heard your prayers and seen your tears (2 Kings 20:5), He's even kept your tears (Psalm 56:8). He will not permit a trusting child of His to sink in the waves of the storm.

Fear not, for I have redeemed you;
I have called you by your name;
You are mine.
When you pass through the waters,
    I will be with you;
And through the rivers,
    they shall not overflow you.
When you walk through the fire,
    you shall not be burned,
Nor shall the flame scorch you.
For I am the Lord your God . . .
you [are] precious in My sight (Isaiah 43:1-4).

The prophet Nahum said: "The Lord is good, a refuge in times of trouble. He cares for those who trust in him" (Nahum 1:7 NIV).

God may not remove you from the scene of battle, but He will be with you in it. God has something better for you than answering your prayers the way you think they should be answered. He is giving you opportunities to trust Him.

This present circumstance which presses so hard against you can be surrendered to Christ. Suffering is the best-shaped tool in the Father's hand to chisel you for life's present realities and for all eternity. Flinch not, then, at what is happening to you. Remember, God transformed the apostle Paul's weakness into strength and his suffering into ultimate glory. We have been left with many biblical illustrations to encourage and help us.

Strange and difficult indeed
    We may find it,
But the blessing that we need
    Is behind it.

The school of suffering produces and graduates rare scholars. Suffering is the tool; character the product. Let your private pain be the doorway into the blessedness that comes from knowing you are in the will of God, and that He has chosen you for this particular experience. He has entrusted you with it.

Ponder this truth: One woman said, "Suffering has been the most creative force in my life. . . . I know now that suffering will last as long as I live, but so will the joy."

Joy out of suffering? A paradox, that the thing we dread the most—suffering and the private pain it usually brings—should be the means to joy. What is that joy? My friend Bob Kilpatrick portrays it in these words:

When wounds become windows,
  and through them we see
  the glory that shall be revealed,
When pain not possessing
  but passing the light
  of joy that cannot be concealed.
When wounds become windows
  clearer than glass,
  and we finally see through the pain,
That all of our suffering
  when counted at last,
  could never amount to our gain
'Til our wounds become windows
  and we see through the pain.

What about your private pain? Could it be divorce, an affair, guilt stemming from abortion, incest, child abuse, hidden drug problems, disappointment in your children, fear, your marriage, low self-esteem? Maybe it's just the monotony of dull routine—this isn't what you imagined for your life back in those days when you nurtured your future dreams. You may be fighting fatigue or a chronic health problem. Perhaps you find yourself confined to a wheelchair or hospital bed; maybe you are in a retirement center, feeling alone and very lonely, seemingly deserted by family and friends. Or perhaps you are not only elderly, but confused, crying out for love, yet rejected by even your caregiver. I am sure that must be very real private pain. Whatever the confines of your circumstances, God is not unmindful of you. Jesus cares.

Amy Carmichael, the amazing woman who served God and suffering humanity, left a comfortable home in England in 1895 to go to India as a missionary. She stayed there for the next 56 years! She risked her life over and over again to rescue little children from the superstitious bondage that destroyed them as "temple servants." In 1931 she suffered a serious fall and for the next 20 years was confined to her room. Imagine it! During that time, she was in constant pain. Yet, she managed the work of the mission and even wrote 13 books! In one of them she wrote:

> We must learn to pray far more for spiritual victory than for protection from battle-wounds, relief from their havoc, rest from their pain. . . . This triumph is not deliverance from pain, but victory in trial, and that not intermittent but perpetual.[7]

You can be sure that this gracious woman would not have chosen to serve God on the mission field from a bed of pain. None of us really wish to suffer. Given our options, we would not choose private pain. But our source of help and encouragement is the Word of God. Our example is Christ "who for the joy that was set before Him endured the cross, despising the shame" (Hebrews 12:2). "For whatever things were written before were written for our learning, that we through the patience and comfort of the Scriptures might have hope" (Romans 15:4).

Never forget that God can make something very good out of something that is or has been very bad and very private. Remember God's answer for Jairus, the synagogue ruler. Consider the father's glad welcome for the prodigal son who found his way home. Bear in mind the apostle Paul's pain, his thorn in the flesh—but remember God's sufficient grace for Paul. And then recall the physical and spiritual healing for that lonely, isolated woman who was caught up in the crowd that followed Jesus. With that dear woman, I desire to say, "If I can but touch the hem of His garment . . ." What about you? For He alone, even Jesus, is our freedom from private pain.

Appendix

In addition to the Scriptures threaded throughout this book, here are additional words of encouragement—some are faith-building, others show God's grace and mercy, and all of them will provide help and hope. (Some of the verses used in the book are repeated here because they are such favorites and provide so much comfort and inspiration.)

"The eternal God is your refuge, and underneath are the everlasting arms" (Deuteronomy 33:27).

"Be strong and of good courage; do not be afraid, nor be dismayed, for the Lord your God is with you wherever you go" (Joshua 1:9).

"For the pillars of the earth are the Lord's, and He has set the world upon them. He will guard the feet of His saints" (1 Samuel 2:8).

"For the Lord will not forsake His people. . . ." (1 Samuel 12:22).

"The Lord your God is gracious and merciful, and will not turn His face from you if you return to Him" (2 Chronicles 30:9).

"The Lord is merciful and gracious, slow to anger, and

abounding in mercy. . . . As a father pities his children, so the Lord pities those who fear Him" (Psalm 103:8,13).

"Whenever I am afraid, I will trust in You. In God (I will praise His word), in God I have put my trust; I will not fear" (Psalm 56:3,4).

"Cast your burden on the Lord, and He shall sustain you. . . ." (Psalm 55:22).

"As for God, His way is perfect; the word of the Lord is proven; He is a shield to all who trust in Him" (Psalm 18:30).

"Even though I walk through the valley of the shadow of death, I will fear no evil, for you are with me; your rod and your staff, they comfort me" (Psalm 23:4 NIV).

"Sing praise to the Lord, you saints of His, and give thanks at the remembrance of His holy name. For His anger is but for a moment, His favor is for life; weeping may endure for a night, but joy comes in the morning" (Psalm 30:4,5).

"I trust in You, O Lord. . . . My times are in Your hands . . . Oh, love the Lord, all you His saints! For the Lord preserves the faithful. . . . Be of good courage, and He shall strengthen your heart, all you who hope in the Lord" (Psalm 31:14,15,23,24).

"Rest in the Lord, and wait patiently for Him; do not fret because of him who prospers in his way, because of the man who brings wicked schemes to pass. . . . Do not fret—it only causes harm. For evildoers shall be cut off. . . ."

". . . the Lord upholds the righteous. . . ."

"For those who are blessed by Him shall inherit the earth. . . . The steps of a good man are ordered by the Lord, and He delights in his way. Though he fall, he shall not be utterly cast down; for the Lord upholds him with His hand."

"For the Lord loves justice, and does not forsake His saints; they are preserved forever. . . ."

"Wait on the Lord, and keep His way . . . the salvation of the righteous is from the Lord; He is their strength in the time of trouble. And the Lord shall help them and deliver them; He shall deliver them from the wicked, and save them, because they trust in Him" (Psalm 37:7-9,17,22-24, 28,34,39,40).

"God is our refuge and strength, a very present help in trouble" (Psalm 46:1).

"You will keep him in perfect peace, whose mind is stayed on You, because he trusts in You" (Isaiah 26:3).

"In quietness and confidence shall be your strength. . . . The Lord is a God of justice; blessed are all those who wait for Him. . . . And though the Lord gives you the bread of adversity and the water of affliction . . . your ears shall hear a word . . . saying, 'This is the way, walk in it. . . .' " (Isaiah 30:15,18,20-21).

"Have you not known? Have you not heard? The everlasting God, the Lord, the Creator of the ends of the earth, neither faints nor is weary. There is no searching of His understanding. He gives power to the weak, and to those who have no might He increases strength. Even the youths shall faint and be weary, and the young men shall utterly fall, but those who wait on the Lord shall renew their strength; they shall mount up with wings like eagles, they

shall run and not be weary, they shall walk and not faint"
(Isaiah 40:28-31).

"I have chosen you and have not cast you away: Fear not,
for I am with you; be not dismayed, for I am your God. I will
strengthen you, yes, I will help you, I will uphold you with
My righteous right hand" (Isaiah 41:9,10).

"When you pass through the waters, I will be with you;
and through the rivers, they shall not overflow you. When
you walk through the fire, you shall not be burned, nor shall
the flame scorch you. For I am the Lord your God, the Holy
One of Israel, your Savior. . . ." (Isaiah 43:2,3).

"For the Lord God will help Me; therefore I will not be
disgraced; therefore I have set My face like a flint, and I
know that I will not be ashamed. He is near who justifies
Me" (Isaiah 50:7,8).

"Listen to Me, you who follow after righteousness, you
who seek the Lord: Look to the rock from which you were
hewn. . . . Listen to Me, you who know righteousness, you
people in whose heart is My law: Do not fear the reproach of
men, nor be afraid of their revilings. For the moth will eat
them up like a garment, and the worm will eat them like
wool; but My righteousness will be forever, and My salvation from generation to generation. . . . So the ransomed
of the Lord shall return . . . they shall obtain joy and gladness, and sorrow and sighing shall flee away. I, even I, am
He who comforts you. Who are you that you should be
afraid. . . . I have put My words in your mouth; I have
covered you with the shadow of My hand . . . You are My
people. Therefore please hear this, you afflicted . . . thus
says your Lord, the Lord and your God, who pleads the
cause of His people: See, I have taken out of your hand the

cup of trembling . . . you shall no longer drink it" (Isaiah 51:1,7,8,11,12,16,21,22).

"Surely He has borne our griefs and carried our sorrows. . . . He was wounded for our transgressions, He was bruised for our iniquities; the chastisement for our peace was upon Him, and by His stripes we are healed. All we like sheep have gone astray; we have turned, every one, to his own way; and the Lord has laid on Him the iniquity of us all" (Isaiah 53:4-6).

"Fear not . . . the reproach of your widowhood you will remember no more. For your husband is your Maker, whose name is the Lord of hosts . . . with great compassion I will gather you. . . . My lovingkindness will not be removed from you. . . . O afflicted one, storm-tossed, and not comforted . . . the well-being of your sons will be great. In righteousness you will be established; you will be far from oppression, for you will not fear; and from terror, for it will not come near you. If anyone fiercely assails you it will not be from Me. Whoever assails you will fall. . . . No weapon that is formed against you shall prosper; and every tongue that accuses you in judgment you will condemn. This is the heritage of the servants of the Lord, and their vindication is from Me, declares the Lord" (Isaiah 54:4,5,7,10,11,13,14, 15,17 NAS).

"The Spirit of the Lord God is upon me, because the Lord has anointed me to bring good news to the afflicted; He has sent me to bind up the brokenhearted, to proclaim liberty to captives, and freedom to prisoners . . . to comfort all who mourn . . . giving them a garland instead of ashes, the oil of gladness instead of mourning, the mantle of praise instead of a spirit of fainting. So they will be called oaks of righteousness, the planting of the Lord, that He may be glorified" (Isaiah 61:1,2,3 NAS).

"Behold, the Lord's hand is not shortened, that it cannot save; nor His ear heavy, that it cannot hear" (Isaiah 59:1).

"Refrain your voice from weeping, and your eyes from tears; for your work shall be rewarded, says the Lord. . . . There is hope in your future, says the Lord" (Jeremiah 31:16,17).

"Do not fear . . . let not your hands be weak. The Lord your God in your midst, the Mighty One, will save; He will rejoice over you with gladness, He will quiet you in His love. . . . (Zephaniah 3:16,17).

"Blessed are the poor in spirit, for theirs is the kingdom of heaven. Blessed are those who mourn, for they shall be comforted. Blessed are the meek, for they shall inherit the earth. Blessed are those who hunger and thirst for righteousness, for they shall be filled. Blessed are the merciful, for they shall obtain mercy. Blessed are the pure in heart, for they shall see God. Blessed are the peacemakers, for they shall be called sons of God. Blessed are those who are persecuted for righteousness' sake, for theirs is the kingdom of heaven. Blessed are you when they revile and persecute you, and say all kinds of evil against you falsely for My sake. Rejoice and be exceedingly glad, for great is your reward in heaven, for so they persecuted the prophets who were before you" (Matthew 5:3-12).

"Daughter, take courage; your faith has made you well" (Matthew 9:22 NAS).

"Come to Me, all you who labor and are heavy laden, and I will give you rest. Take My yoke upon you and learn from Me, for I am gentle and lowly in heart, and you will find rest for your souls. For My yoke is easy and My burden is light" (Matthew 11:28-30).

"He who is without sin among you, let him throw a stone at her first. . . . Woman, where are those accusers of yours? Has no one condemned you?" She said, "No one, Lord." And Jesus said to her, "Neither do I condemn you; go and sin no more."

Then Jesus spoke to them again, saying, "I am the light of the world. He who follows Me shall not walk in darkness, but have the light of life" (John 8:7,10-12).

"Peace I leave with you, My peace I give to you; not as the world gives do I give to you. Let not your heart be troubled, neither let it be afraid" (John 14:27).

"The Spirit . . . helps in our weaknesses. For we do not know what we should pray for as we ought, but the Spirit Himself makes intercession for us with groanings which cannot be uttered. . . . And we know that all things work together for good to those who love God, to those who are the called according to His purpose" (Romans 8:26,28).

"If God is for us, who can be against us?. . . Who shall bring a charge against God's elect? It is God who justifies. . . . Who shall separate us from the love of Christ? Shall tribulation, or distress, or persecution, or famine, or nakedness, or peril, or sword?. . . Yet in all these things we are more than conquerors through Him who loved us. For I am persuaded that neither death nor life, nor angels nor principalities nor powers, nor things present nor things to come, nor height nor depth, nor any other created thing, shall be able to separate us from the love of God which is in Christ Jesus our Lord" (Romans 8:31,33,35,37-39).

"And He said to me, 'My grace is sufficient for you, for My strength is made perfect in weakness'" (2 Corinthians 12:9).

"Finally, my brethren, be strong in the Lord and in the power of His might. Put on the whole armor of God, that you may be able to stand against the wiles of the devil. For we do not wrestle against flesh and blood, but against principalities, against powers, against the rulers of the darkness of this age, against spiritual hosts of wickedness in the heavenly places. Therefore take up the whole armor of God, that you may be able to withstand in the evil day, and having done all, to stand. Stand therefore, having girded your waist with truth, having put on the breastplate of righteousness, and having shod your feet with the preparation of the gospel of peace; above all, taking the shield of faith with which you will be able to quench all the fiery darts of the wicked one. And take the helmet of salvation, and the sword of the Spirit, which is the word of God; praying always with all prayer and supplication in the spirit. . . ." (Ephesians 6:10-18).

"For to you it has been granted on behalf of Christ, not only to believe in Him, but also to suffer for His sake" (Philippians 1:29).

"My God shall supply all your need according to His riches in glory by Christ Jesus" (Philippians 4:19).

"The Lord is faithful, who will establish you and guard you from the evil one" (2 Thessalonians 3:3).

"For whatever God says to us is full of living power. . . . Jesus the Son of God is our great High Priest who has gone to heaven itself to help us; therefore let us never stop trusting him. This High Priest of ours understands our weaknesses, since he had the same temptations we do, though he never once gave way to them and sinned. So let us come boldly to the very throne of God and stay there to receive his mercy and to find grace to help us in our times of need" (Hebrews 4:12,14-16 TLB).

"Let us draw near with a true heart in full assurance of faith. . . . Let us hold fast the confession of our hope without wavering, for He who promised is faithful" (Hebrews 10:22,23).

"Consider Him who endured such opposition from sinful men, so that you will not grow weary and lose heart. My son, do not make light of the Lord's discipline, and do not lose heart when he rebukes you, because the Lord disciplines those he loves, and he punishes everyone he accepts as a son. Endure hardship as discipline; God is treating you as sons. . . . No discipline seems pleasant at the time, but painful. Later on, however, it produces a harvest of righteousness and peace for those who have been trained by it" (Hebrews 12:3,5,7,11 NIV).

"Draw near to God and He will draw near to you" (James 4:8).

"My brethren, take the prophets, who spoke in the name of the Lord, as an example of suffering and patience. Indeed we count them blessed who endure. You have heard of the preserverance of Job and seen the end intended by the Lord—that the Lord is very compassionate and merciful" (James 5:10,11).

"Dear friends, do not be surprised at the painful trial you are suffering, as though something strange were happening to you. But rejoice that you participate in the sufferings of Christ, so that you may be overjoyed when his glory is revealed. . . . If you suffer as a Christian, do not be ashamed, but praise God that you bear that name. . . . Humble yourselves, therefore, under God's mighty hand, that he may lift you up in due time. Cast all your anxiety on him because he cares for you" (1 Peter 4:12,13,16; 5:6,7 NIV).

Notes

Chapter 1—The Pain We Don't Talk About

1. Warren W. Wiersbe, *Why Us? When Bad Things Happen to God's People* (Revell, 1984), p. 86.

Chapter 2—The Insignificant Factor

1. Emile Cailliet, *Alone at High Noon* (Zondervan, 1971), p. 87.
2. Harry Blamires, *A God Who Acts* (Servant Books, 1957), p. 19.
3. Ibid., p. 20.

Chapter 3—The Risk Factor

1. Wayne E. Oates, *Nurturing Silence in a Noisy Heart* (Doubleday Galilee Original, 1979), p. 97.

Chapter 4—The Despair Factor

1. G. Campbell Morgan, *Studies in the Four Gospels* (Revell, 1931), p. 94.
2. Ibid.
3. Paul Tournier, *Escape from Loneliness* (Westminster Press, 1972), p. 27.

Chapter 5—The Bondage Factor

1. C. S. Lewis, *The Problem of Pain* (MacMillan, 1962), p. 93.
2. Vernon E. Johnson, *I'll Quit Tomorrow* (Harper & Row, 1980), pp. 116-17.
3. Lewis, op. cit., pp. 93, 95, 97.
4. Helen Hosier, *You Never Stop Being a Parent* (Revell, 1986), pp. 146-47. Mrs. Hosier urges those needing help with alcoholism to call The Johnson Institute for more information:

Toll-free 1-800-231-5165; in Minnesota, 1-800-247-0484.

Also, check locally for programs that provide intervention information and help. Many people have been helped through Alcoholics Anonymous. Look in your Yellow Pages for local information.

5. Ibid., p. 152.
6. John Powell, *He Touched Me*, pp. 86-87.
7. Ibid., pp. 87-88.
8. Ibid., p. 85.

Chapter 6—The Guilt Factor
1. Dwight Carlson, *From Guilt to Grace* (Harvest House, 1983), Preface.
2. Ibid., p. 52.
3. A. W. Tozer, *I Talk Back to the Devil* (Christian Publications, 1972), pp. 9-10, 12.
4. Ibid., p. 21.
5. Carlson, op. cit., p. 122.
6. Hosier, op. cit., p. 67.
7. If the problem of homosexuality is an issue in your family, or with someone you know and love, Barbara Johnson's ministry is being used nationwide by the Lord to help scrape people off the ceiling (where they land when they learn that someone dear to them has this problem). That's why she called her ministry "Spatula Ministries." She can be reached at P.O. Box 444, La Habra, CA 90631. Phone: (213)691-7369.

Chapter 7—The Dragon Factor
1. Marilee Zdenek and Marge Champion, from *God is a Verb!* as cited by Mary Franzen Clark in her book *Hiding, Hurting, Healing* (Zondervan, 1985), p. 133.
2. Betty Esses DeBlase, *Survivor of a Tarnished Ministry* (Truth Publishers, P.O. Box 3585, Orange, CA 92665). For counseling requests, comments, inquiries, or copies of the book, send to address listed.
3. Stephen D. Eyre, *Defeating the Dragons of the World* (InterVarsity Press, 1987), p. 17.

Chapter 8—Paindrops Keep Falling
1. Juanita R. Ryan, *Standing By* (Tyndale, 1984), p. 102.

2. Powell, op. cit., p. 30.
3. Ibid., p. 67.
4. Robert M. Herhold, *The Promise Beyond the Pain* (Abingdon, 1979), p. 27.
5. Ibid., p. 106.
6. Mrs. Chas. E. Cowman, *Streams In the Desert* (Cowman Publishing Co., 1950), pp. 178-79.
7. Ibid., p. 65.

Chapter 9—Oh, the Thorns!

1. Charles R. Swindoll, *Come Before Winter* (Multnomah Press, 1985), p. 325.
2. Cowman, op. cit., pp. 239-40.
3. Herhold, op. cit., p. 97.
4. Perry Tanksley, *Love Gift* (Revell, 1971), p. 46.

Chapter 10—Suffering the Tool; Character the Product

1. Wiersbe, op. cit., pp. 115, 120.
2. Ibid., p. 116.
3. Ibid., p. 116.
4. Helen Hosier, *Living Cameos* (Revell, 1984), p. 11.
5. Oswald Chambers, *My Utmost for His Highest* (Dodd, Mead & Co., 1963), p. 306.
6. Ibid., p. 306.
7. Wiersbe, p. 121.

Other Books by Rich Wilkerson

Teenagers: Parental Guidance Suggested

Carnal Christians and Other Words That
Don't Go Together

Straight Answers to Tough Questions about Sex

For further information regarding Rich Wilkerson Crusades, please write:

Rich Wilkerson
P.O. Box 1092
Tacoma, WA 98401

OTHER GOOD
HARVEST HOUSE READING

BLOW AWAY THE BLACK CLOUDS
by *Florence Littauer*

Florence Littauer helps the reader come to terms with the emotional handicap of depression, offers practical insight on how to determine the cause—physical, psychological, or spiritual—and maps out the guidelines for constructive action to overcome depression.

BOUNCING BACK
Finding Acceptance in the Face of Rejection
by *William Coleman*

Rejection is coming, just like bad weather! How we cope with its devastating effects will mean the difference between success and failure in our lives. Bestselling author William Coleman explores with sensitivity and insight such topics as: types of rejection, preparing your children to handle rejection, self-rejection, bouncing back when you feel you can't. Coleman's compassionate approach and godly counsel will help you turn the hurt of rejection into building blocks for a healthy self-image.

FREEDOM FROM GUILT
by *Bruce Narramore* and *Bill Counts*

Silent condemnation cripples and enslaves many sensitive Christians. But there is freedom from both depression and fear of failure. The authors combine their insights to illuminate the path of complete forgiveness and self-acceptance.

HOW TO WIN OVER FEAR
by *John Haggai*

Fear is a pervasive and destructive influence in modern society. Everyone seems to be afraid of something. Dr. John Haggai explores the different types of fears, the essential prerequisites and formula for winning over fear, and God's power that is available to conquer fear.

HOW TO WIN OVER PAIN
by *John Haggai*

With the same clear insight and powerful answers that made *How to Win Over Worry* a bestseller for more than 20 years, John Haggai addresses the problem of pain in our lives. Covering the gamut from physical suffering to the emotional anguish of rejection, loneliness, death, or separation, *How to Win Over Pain* asks the hard questions of life and presents God's strong and loving answers to our hurt and pain.

HOW TO WIN OVER WORRY
by *John Haggai*

People need help in overcoming worry and need it desperately. The worry problem is at the root of much domestic strife, business failure, economic crises, incurable sicknesses, and premature deaths—to mention but a few of worry's hazards. Presenting more than a diagnosis, Dr. Haggai shows how God's Word offers the prescription for worry that can rid us of worry's devastating effects forever.

OVERCOMING HURTS AND ANGER
by *Dr. Dwight Carlson*

Dr. Carlson shows us how to confront our feelings and negative emotions in order to experience liberation and fulfillment. He presents seven practical steps to help us identify and cope with our feelings of hurt and anger.

THE PURPOSE OF SUFFERING
Knowing the God Who Comforts
by *Dr. H. Edwin Young*

A recent Gallup poll revealed that the most frequently asked question in America is "Why do people suffer?" Dr. H. Edwin Young takes the reader through the book of Job for God's answer. He rejects the simplistic doctrines prevalent today that state, "You are suffering because of sin. . . . God is punishing you!" and "As a child of God you can have complete health, wealth, and success just for the asking." Instead, he points the way to the sovereign God who alone can comfort us and show us *The Purpose of Suffering*.